CHINT SINGH

THE MAN WHO
SHOULD HAVE DIED

*A captivating true World War 2 story of an Indian POW, the sole
survivor out of more than 2500 men, rescued by Australian defence
forces in the jungles of New Guinea and became the chief witness in the
Australian War Crimes Commission*

NARINDER SINGH PARMAR

Printed in Australia

Cover Design by Shawline Publishing Group

First Printing: Sept 2021 Australia

Shawline Publishing Group Pty Ltd
www.shawlinepublishing.com.au

Paperback ISBN- 9781922444608
Ebook ISBN- 9781922444615

Dedication

This book is dedicated to all Indian soldiers who sacrificed their lives in the line of duty in Papua and New Guinea; the natives of Papua and New Guinea and Australian Defence forces who rescued Chint Singh and his 10 men and showed them a new life and fostered the Anzac spirit of courage, comradeship and justice.

CONTENTS

FOREWORD

Narinder Singh Parmar's book *Chint Singh: The Man Who Should Have Died* tells an extraordinary and moving story, one which all interested in Australia's part in the Second World War should know, and one that assumes an even greater significance now that Indian migrants form an increasingly important proportion of those whom Australia welcomes.

Jemadar Chint Singh, a junior officer in the 2/12th Frontier Force Regiment, had been one of the 45,000 troops of the Indian Army captured in the fall of Singapore in 1942. From mid-1943 to the end of September 1945 he was part of the Indian POW working parties shipped to New Guinea. Singh was one of the very few survivors of one of the most extreme experiences of captivity in the entire world war. Chint Singh himself was the only survivor of the 560 men of his 16th POW Working Party.

Statistically, Chint Singh should have died as a prisoner. That he survived was partly due to luck, but also to the comradeship he shared with his fellow POWs, the relationships he formed with the people of New Guinea (who were also oppressed by the occupying Japanese), and by the resilience he found within himself, as the story he tells in this powerful story of survival.

So remote was the New Guinea coast that it was a full six weeks after the formal end of hostilities that Chint Singh was at last liberated by Australian forces. The day he met the Australians, he writes, was the day on which he was 'reborn' (a characteristically Indian way to express his feelings of gratitude). The notable feature of this part of Chint Singh's story is the way in which he was greeted and treated by men who had grown up in a self-consciously and officially 'white' Australia. But, as his account testifies, they regarded him as a fellow officer, and he never forgot their respect and friendship.

On 15 November 1945 a Dakota transport carrying ten of Chint Singh's liberated comrades crashed while carrying them homeward, killing all on board. Chint Singh would probably have been among them, but his testimony was needed in the trials of Japanese soldiers charged with war crimes. Again, he was the man who should have died.

Biographies of fathers by sons are hardly unknown in Australian military history, but this book is an act of filial piety with a South Asian inflexion. Much of the story is told in Chint Singh's own words, recounted with a simple, factual dignity in which his personality shines through: a clue to why Australians in 1945 found him such an appealing character.

The friendships which Chint Singh forged in 1945 changed the life of his family. Chint Singh himself returned to Australia and Papua New Guinea in 1970, renewing friendships while remembering those lost in the war. His son Narinder Singh Parmar, as he relates in this book, migrated to Australia, becoming a teacher, because of his father's affection for the country that had led to his 'rebirth'.

The story Narinder Singh Parmar has compiled, is remarkable in many ways: because autobiographies by men of the old Indian Army are rare, because it documents one of the most appalling experiences of privation, hardship and death notable not just in Indian or in Australian military history, but on a global scale. But above all, because Chint Singh truly was The Man Who Should Have Died.

Prof. Peter Stanley
UNSW Canberra

Acknowledgements

My first and principal debt is to my father Chint Singh and mother Kalawati, whose blessings have allowed me to complete this project. Though at times I felt disoriented and questions of self-doubt crept in, however, the values that my parents inculcated in me helped me to reach at this point to publish this book. I must admit that somewhere, deep in my heart, I had the feeling that my father's soul had assigned me to tell his and his mates' story to the world, something which he wanted to do. It is a matter of honour,which I feel I have done.

I am grateful to Mr Kevin Deutrum, who was in government service in Papua and New Guinea for a long time and saw many Indian soldiers' resting places in various cemeteries. During his tenure there, he found a memorial that was dedicated to Chint Singh and his fallen men, in 1971. I met him in Brisbane in 1990 when he stopped by, while on his way to his hometown, Adelaide. Our meeting surely sowed the seed in my mind to work on my father's amazing survival story.

It was an honour and immense humbling experience to meet late

R.A.N. officer Marsden Hordern, whom my father called him with his nickname 'Tony'. Marsden Hordern was the naval commander of the patrol boat Q1347 and rescued Chint Singh and his 10 mates in 1945. Marsden Hordern and Chint Singh became good friends and they cherished this friendship for the rest of their lives. In his book, 'A Merciful Journey', Marsden Hordern has shared about his meeting with Chint Singh.

My gratitude goes to Ian McNamara, ABC radio host of Sunday program Australia All Over who interviewed me in 2002 about my father's story. Following this program, I had an overwhelming response from all over Australia by people who encouraged me to tell Chint Singh's story. That opportunity also allowed me to reconnect with some of the families who knew Chint Singh and met him. This set me to travel and meet many families in Canberra, Melbourne, Caloundra, Perth and Sydney.

My special thanks to late Lieutenant F.O. Monk, who shared part of his memoir when he was on the Australian rescue party up the Sepik River and he, for the first time, met Chint Singh and his other 10 Indian soldiers. I did not meet him in person, though I had a brief conversation over the phone with him and he told me he will share his memory of meeting Chint Singh for the first time. I have included his account in this book.

I was honoured to meet Professor Peter Stanley who has done extensive research on Indian POWs, including Chint Singh. Professor Stanley has been my mentor during the completion of this manuscript, and I am incredibly grateful to him to write a 'foreword' for this book.

My thanks also go to Adil Chhina for his editorial assistance. He is a freelance military, historical researcher and editor specialising in the history of the Indian Army. He has previously worked for the United Service Institution of India, Centre for Armed Forces Historical Research and the Commonwealth War Graves Commission in New Delhi. He is presently completing an MA in War, Media and Society at the University of Kent.

I am thankful to Jonathon Dallimore, research historian who has always been there to provide me with his feedback on short notice. Finally, I would like to thank my children, Nakul and Mohini, who have been checking on me about the progress of this project. Much appreciate their constant motivation.

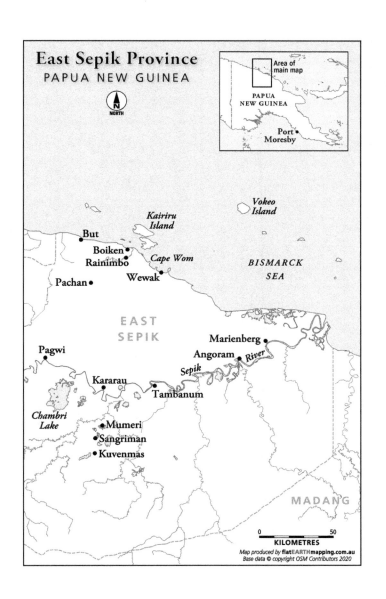

East Sepik Province
PAPUA NEW GUINEA

NORTH

Area of main map

PAPUA NEW GUINEA

Port Moresby

Vokeo Island

Kairiru Island

But
Boiken
Rainimbo
Cape Wom
Pachan
Wewak

BISMARCK SEA

EAST SEPIK

Marienberg
Angoram
River
Pagwi
Sepik
Kararau
Tambanum

Chambri Lake
Mumeri
Sangriman
Kuvenmas

MADANG

0   50
KILOMETRES

Map produced by flatEARTHmapping.com.au
Base data © copyright OSM Contributors 2020

INTRODUCTION

"DAD SERIOUS. GO home and bring mummy to Lucknow." This was the telegram I received from my eldest brother, Col. S.S. Parmar, (then Major) who was posted at Military Hospital, Lucknow, where Dad was being treated for a urinary issue, and eventually it was found he had prostate cancer. At the time, I was based in Chandigarh and teaching in a private institute.

When I reached Lucknow, mother and I were driven straight to the Military Hospital. We approached his bed and saw he had an oxygen mask on and was breathing heavy. My mother held his hand and said something like "I am here" or "I have reached here" in her native language. There was no response. She raised her voice and kept repeating herself, and I could see her pain and anguish. We were told he had gone into a coma just a day ago and had not recovered. We then left for my brother's home. I would visit every day after that and around the 4th day he died during the early hours of 13th February 1983.

In these four days, I used to sit next to his bed and just reflect on his life. The nurses who took care of him told me he shared his war stories. He was cremated at the banks of the river Gomti with full army honour.

Who was Chint Singh? I came to know more about his World War Two story after his death. I was aware of his days as a prisoner of war during World War Two and his links with his Australian friends. However, I experienced true Australian mateship after migrating to Australia in 1989.

After almost spending 11 years in Brisbane, I moved to Broken Hill, New South Wales, as a high school teacher. In August 2002, I was interviewed on Radio National ABC (Macca's show on Sundays- Australia All Over) regarding my father's story. After the interview, the response I received was absolutely amazing. I was able to contact Australian World War Two veterans who knew or had met my father. I was humbled by their support and kind words. At times, sitting alone contemplating my father's story and the responses I received, I would look up at the skies and say, "Dad, I have experienced true Australian mateship, which you did during the war." This began my journey to meet those old links my father had. Luckily for me, he had put together his story in his own words, which he wanted the world to know.

Boyhood to overseas deployment

Chint Singh was born on 15th March 1917 in a village called Tillu in the district of Hamirpur, in undivided Punjab (now Himachal Pradesh), India. The village lies in the foothills of the Himalayas. His family had migrated there from the Dhar region in Central India. He was a Rajput and belonged to the *Kshatriya* or warrior caste.

His father, Sain Das, had inherited large tracts of land as he was the only child of his parents. He owned seventy acres of land, which were cultivated by tenants. Being a high-class Rajput, it was considered beneath his dignity to plough the land himself. He had farm labourers or servants employed to work on the farm. Chint's mother, like all other womenfolk of the time, lived within the confines of the house looking after household affairs. Chint was the youngest among his siblings. He had four brothers and a sister. By the time he grew up, the family was well settled and had a good income from the farm as well as the family business. This gave him the opportunity to finish his education and attend college. In those days, it was uncommon for Indians from rural backgrounds to have a college education.

Chint Singh was brought up in a very disciplined environment. He recalls in one of his notes "My father was a very tough person and a good organiser…mother was an excellent administrator, economist and a leader amongst the women of the area."

Being the youngest in the family, Chint was a favourite and perhaps spoilt too. He once asked his father to buy him a pony and sure enough, he got it. He was so excited with the pony that he started riding it without a saddle and used small ropes for reins. He soon realised this was not a good idea, as he became sore for two weeks. His upbringing and his love for outdoor activities had a great impact on his life. He writes "…I used to hunt birds with stones, collect some dry wood and roast the bird and eat it while sharing it with my companions. The same applied for fish. I seldom used to carry fish home but would smoke them on the fire or bake them wrapped in tree leaves and eat them without any spices or salt." He did not realise that one day all this would stand him in good stead when his destiny would take him to the jungles of New Guinea.

He started schooling at the age of six. He was an average student but good at sports and other activities like drama, leadership, and management. Fishing and hunting were his favourite hobbies. He spent most of his time engaged in sports and hobbies rather than his studies. He was on his school hockey team and continued to play hockey in college as well. He disliked mathematics, but loved both geography and history. He also participated in debates, poetry recitation and public speaking. He completed his high school at a boarding school in Hamirpur. The school was in a hilly and heavily forested area, which gave him the opportunity to continue his outdoor activities like bush walking and trekking. He used to go out on the small rolling hills and study there.

He would recite his lessons, stories and poems in a loud voice to the trees. He had a special love for nature, which later proved handy during his captivity in New Guinea. It seems that destiny was working to shape and prepare him for the conditions he would face later in his life.

After finishing high school, he went to the D.A.V. College in Hoshiarpur, Punjab, to continue his education. This town was forty-three miles from his village. The journey had to be made on foot. This was the first time he saw trains, buses, and cars. Town life was very different and novel for him, but he adjusted quickly.

While he was in college, his father died at the age of 58. He was very disheartened and found it hard to bear the loss of his father, who was close to him. This loss affected his studies at college. To make things worse, in December 1933, he had an attack of rheumatism and suffered severely for three months. He eventually graduated from college in 1934.

Joining the army

There was great turmoil and unemployment at the time. Chint, however, had always wanted to join the army, so he had decided he would give that his best shot. He had a few options. He could enter the Indian Military Academy as a cadet and get commissioned as an officer, or enlist through the ranks. He sought help from some of his relatives who were already serving in the army. He decided to choose the latter route. In November 1934, he appeared before a recruiting officer who found him unfit as he did not meet the physical requirements. The required chest measurement was 32-34 inches and he measured 31-33 inches. However, he was not disheartened by this setback and instead took it as a challenge. He started exercising regularly and his mother arranged for a special diet for him. After four months of hard work, he became fitter and healthier and could run a mile in good time. He went back to the recruiting office and got through his second attempt.

After being accepted, he was sent to the Frontier Force Regiment Training Centre in Sialkot (now in Pakistan). He appeared before

Major Barronet, a company commander in the 2nd Battalion of the12th Frontier Force Regiment. Major Barronet checked Chint Singh's physical standards and proficiency at games and racing, after which he recommended him for the medical examination. Chint was declared fit for service and enrolled as a sepoy on 23rd August 1935 at a pay scale of 50/- rupees per month.

Training days

The training of recruits was very rigorous and lasted eleven months. It included drills with the rifle and bayonet as well as section and platoon battle drills. Most recruits had little education, and many were illiterate. The instructors were not fond of educated boys who joined the army, as they could later stand in the way of promotion. Corporal punishment of recruits was very common though not given in the presence of British officers and any instructor seen or reported to have beaten a recruit was charge-sheeted and punished under the Indian Army Act. In the chain of command, all the regimental officers from company commanders up to the post of commandants were British officers, the platoon commanders and company second-in-commands were Indian Viceroy's Commissioned Officers (VCOs) and below them were Indian instructors. The training staff and VCOs were the creme de la creme of a regiment. Their turn-out, smartness and physical fitness was a model for all to follow. It was considered a privilege to be trained by such professional, smart and zealous instructors.

After his arrival at the barracks, Chint Singh was guided to a military tailor to get his uniform fitted. He was also given mufti clothing to be worn on special occasions, such as the pay parade, to visit the town or to attend a function. In his diary he writes, "I was also issued a cot and wooden box to store my kit. I was then handed over to Lance-Naik (L/Nk) Onkar Chand, my line section commander, who gave me a long lecture on dos and don'ts." After getting all the required instructions, Chint then began preparations for the next day, which included polishing his boots and leather belt and learning how to tie his turban in the military fashion.

The following day, he reported to his platoon commander, Naik (Nk) Mohinder Singh, who gave him some instructions and then handed him over to the section commander L/Nk Painda Khan, who was responsible for his training. There were nine new recruits in his section who had begun their training a month earlier. However, L/Nk Khan helped Chint Singh to catch up with the other boys. L/Nk Khan made an ever-lasting impression on Chint. He was so impressed by Khan's training, leadership qualities, professionalism and personality that Chint made him his role model. Painda Khan's section was so well trained that it always came first in drill competitions. Chint was also proud of his own achievements and performance. It was a custom in the Frontier Force Regiment that if a recruit obtained first position in firing and was recommended by the drill and physical training instructor, he was awarded a purple-coloured chevron to be worn on the right sleeve of the shirt. Chint Singh had been proud to earn that distinction.

Besides drill and physical training, the recruits had to go through regular classes in Roman Urdu, Roman Hindi[1], English and map-reading. Chint scored high grades in these subjects and consequently was appointed education instructor to teach Roman Urdu to other recruits. His teaching ability earned him the title of *masterji* or teacher.

After thirty-six weeks of training, he went home on two weeks' leave. His mother and family were happy to see him turning into a well-built and smart young man. After the leave was over, he returned to the training centre to be inducted as a sepoy in the British Indian Army. Chint maintained a diary throughout his career in the army. It is his accounts in these diaries which are reproduced in the following pages that give us a glimpse into his life and his time in captivity.

So here is the story of Chint Singh, as narrated by him in his diaries and documents.

---

1   Urdu and Hindi written in Roman script.

CHAPTER I
BRITISH INDIAN ARMY

ON THE LAST Saturday of July 1936, we took an oath of loyalty by touching the King's colours, the regimental colours and our religious books. We swore allegiance to our King and country and to obey all orders issued by superior officers even at the peril of our lives.

Thus ended the first very difficult part of my service in the army. It had a tremendous effect on my future. I could say I was turned into a perfect soldier by my instructors. I learnt more during my training than I had in my 12 years of education in school and college. As far as the British officers' behaviour and treatment were concerned, it differed from person to person.

Trained soldier

After the attestation parade was over, I bid farewell to my recruit's dress, which I had worn for about eleven months and changed over to the trained soldier's uniform. As was customary, I distributed sweets to the men in my barracks and other friends on becoming a full-fledged sepoy. The next day, we were marched before the company commander. He told me that I had a good future, provided that I continue to work hard in the battalion.

The next day, we left Sialkot and were drafted to our respective battalions. I was posted to the 2nd Battalion, 12th Frontier Force Regiment (2/12 FFR), then located at Chaman in Baluchistan. It was a very thrilling but long train journey which lasted three days. We travelled via Lahore, Multan and Quetta to Chaman. We were received at the railway station by the duty VCO and were ordered to load our luggage onto mule carts, which was the authorised unit transport in those days. We marched behind the carts to the barracks in the fort and were assigned to different companies. I was posted to 'A' company which had no company commander. The senior VCO, Subedar Rai Singh[2], was my platoon commander and was also the officiating company commander. The following day, the new drafts were presented before the adjutant, Captain Campbell Patrick Murray[3]. He told me he was very happy to see my service record from the training centre and advised me to keep it up. Then we were seen by the commanding officer (CO) Lieutenant-Colonel HGA Pearson[4]. He also spoke a few words of encouragement.

Cadre Training

One day, the company commander told me I was required by the adjutant in the Battalion Headquarters to undergo a cadre for instructorship. I was one of twelve soldiers selected for this course. Some of them had been training continuously for six months for instructorship. To be an instructor in drill and weapons training was considered to be a

---

2   Rai Singh enlisted in the army on 10th April 1916 and was directly commissioned as a VCO. A veteran of the First World War, he had served in Mesopotamia, Waziristan in 1924 and on the North-West Frontier of India in 1930.

3   C. P. Murray was commissioned in the Indian army on 1st February 1932. He had been adjutant of the battalion since July 1933.

4   Lt-Col Pearson was commissioned in the Indian army on 9th September 1908. He had been appointed as the commandant of the battalion on 20th February 1934.

most prized job and a ladder for promotion to lance-naik and higher. My instructors were happy with my performance. Days went by quickly and I qualified to become an instructor.

I did not return to my company and stayed at the training centre to train other soldiers. My papers were sent to the military district headquarters at Quetta for further promotion. I started visualising becoming a cadet and then a commissioned officer in the army. Destiny, however, did not favour me and the papers were sent back, stating I would be over age by a month at the start of the course. The CO, adjutant and second-in-command saw me informally in their office and expressed their concern.

In the spring of 1938, the battalion moved to Lansdowne. Lansdowne is a hill station in the western part of the United Provinces (now Uttaranchal). The battalion settled down to peace time training. I was again called on to the battalion training team to give training in weapons to two young British officers and two senior non-commissioned officers (NCOs). It was another feather in my cap to be delegated to train British officers while I was still a sepoy.

Marriage

My mother had meanwhile arranged my marriage, so she wrote to me to come home. As was the custom in those days, I did not know, and had never seen, Kalawati (my wife) before our marriage. The marriage celebrations lasted for six days. She was too shy to talk to me. We got married on 11th August 1938. She was only sixteen years old and I was twenty-one. I went back to my battalion, a married man without ever having talked to her.

War breaks out

The battalion had hardly settled down after the annual training camp and presentation of regimental colours by the Viceroy of India, Lord Linlithgow, that orders were received to move to Waziristan in the

North-West Frontier Province to take part in the operations there.[5] I was, however, posted to the training centre at Sialkot as a drill instructor.

In July 1939, I was detailed to attend a senior instructor's course in the Army School of Education at Belgaum. The course was for teaching English to army personnel. It was an interesting and useful course but unfortunately, I could not complete it as the Second World War broke out in September 1939. I was posted back to my battalion, which was now located near Peshawar. As a result of the war, Indian forces were sent to fight overseas. This led to an increased recruitment in the Indian Army. There were two more battalions added to my regiment, which lead to promotion avenues for me. I appeared in the promotion cadre and achieved a distinction which gave me my first promotion to lance/naik on 5th June 1940.

In the meantime, we got some new British officers from England. One of them was Lieutenant (Lt) Sedgwick. He was very intelligent, but did not know any Urdu[6]. He used to observe me teaching English to the soldiers. We both developed close relations and both of us learnt much from one another. I learnt English from him, and he learnt Roman Urdu from me.

Promotion

One day the adjutant, under whom I had been conducting the training and English classes, called me and asked whether I would mind going as an instructor in drill and weapons training to the Army Signal Training Centre at Jabalpur. I agreed and the adjutant discussed my case with other junior officers. I was subsequently asked to pack up and move to Jabalpur after being promoted to the rank of naik. I arrived at the training centre on 16th August 1940 and reported for duty. I was given a platoon of forty-five new recruits and three instructors to help me.

---

5   An insurrection at the end of February 1933 broke out in Southern Afghanistan. A few frontier tribes crossed the Afghan border in the hopes of looting the area and a cordon of troops (including the 2/12 FFR) were sent to deal with the movement of these tribesmen.

6   Urdu was the *lingua-franca* of the Indian Army

All those recruits were from South India. They could not understand any other language except English and their own South-Indian language – Telegu. It was quite a difficult task to deal with them, but I managed it and the senior officers were happy to see the performance. Consequently, I was promoted to lance-havildar. In February 1941, my battalion moved near Quetta in Baluchistan in preparation to move on an overseas deployment while I was stationed at the Signals Training Centre.

Overseas deployment

On 14th February 1941, I received a telegram from my regiment advising me to join it forthwith for overseas service. At the Signals Training Centre, I was a well-known instructor. Hence, when orders came for my departure, the adjutant and the training staff were very sorry to see me go. My wife, Kalawati, who had been with me for the last three months, was very grieved over the sudden news. We packed our baggage on 15th February and bid farewell to the centre.

On 18th February, I left my wife back at the village and departed for an unknown experience and for an unknown period. We never imagined the war would go on for five years. More importantly, we had no idea we would not see each other again for three and a half years.

I joined my unit on 21st February, and after a few weeks, the regiment, under the command of Lt-Col A.E. Cumming MC, moved to Secunderabad where we underwent intense training until we were ready for overseas service. We left Secunderabad on 9th April and went to Madras (now Chennai) where we loaded our luggage onto a ship called the 'Ashanthia'. On 11th April, I said goodbye to my mother-country and saluted her from the deck of the ship, not knowing what my destiny would be or what changes might come over me and my country before I would see it again. The war then was in the west and we had no idea where we were going. Every movement was kept very secret on account of spies. After two days of sailing east, I began to think our destination must be in the Far East. On the third day, we were officially informed we were going to Malaya. We were given many lectures on the geographical conditions of the country and everyone was feeling happy we were not going to the desert.

On 16th April, I had my first look at the big island. There were many boats sailing in the sea but they were very small, being manned by one or two men each. This was a new experience for us, although we had been told the Malayan natives go out in the sea to fish. The ship entered the harbour of Penang in the afternoon and anchored far from the shore. We were taken ashore by small steamers. This journey was my first experience at sea, and I enjoyed it very much even though I was slightly sea sick.

After the landing, we moved to Taiping by train. I noticed a big difference between the trains of India and Malaya. The accommodation was very nice and comfortable. When we reached Taiping, I knew I would like it very much as the scenery and climate were very good. The inhabitants were mostly Malayans and Chinese and they looked very smart when dressed in clean clothes, particularly the Chinese. At Taiping, there were many Indians consisting of Sikhs from Punjab and others from southern India.

After a few months' stay in Taiping, the regiment was ordered to move to Kota Bharu. At Kota Bharu, we were very busy in preparing the defences of that area. In spite of this, the soldiers were happy, and the letters home were full of good news relating to food, clothing, pay and recreations. The rations were excellent. We were provided with Australian sheep for mutton, tinned fruits and tinned milk. None of us had the slightest idea of the terrible time which lay ahead.

The Japanese bombing of Kota Bharu, Singapore Island and all the important places on the Malayan Peninsula on the nights of 7th and 8th December 1941 was very sudden. At the same time, they landed in many places and started to overrun the country. My battalion distinguished itself at several places and was the first to win the Victoria Cross, followed by several other decorations. In spite of the stiff resistance put up by the Allies, the Japanese, who were well equipped and in superior numbers, managed to get into Singapore. The fall of Singapore on 15th February 1942 was a deadly blow to the Allied forces, whose fate was sealed in the inhuman hands of the Japanese. Life was in chaos and there was disorder everywhere. It was very hard to decide one's own fate. Our gallant soldiers were turned into coolies and forced labourers by the Japanese and were subjected to daily torture. Arrangements for rations, medical aid and sanitary measures were handled very badly by the Japanese.

The occupation of Singapore by the Japanese was completed within a month. The spread of disease, starvation and ill-treatment brought about many deaths every day. Civilians too, were badly treated. The women especially were tortured, insulted, and raped by the Japanese. Allied officers and soldiers were beaten while doing fatigues. The prisoners of war (POWs) used to say it would have been better to have been killed on the battlefield than to be slapped, beaten and insulted by such an inhuman race.

In April 1943, about 5,000 Indian POWs were ordered away from the island of Singapore by the Japanese. We all hoped for the best but did not realise the worst days were yet to come. We were put aboard cargo boats on 5th May 1943 and sailed again for an unknown destination.

Chint Singh – Boyhood

Chint Singh at Army Headquarters, Melbourne, May 1947

Chint Singh, Singapore, 1941

An Infantry battalion on duty at Khojak Pass, Chaman, Pakistan (then NWFP), July 1936. Chint Singh is 2nd from left, front row.

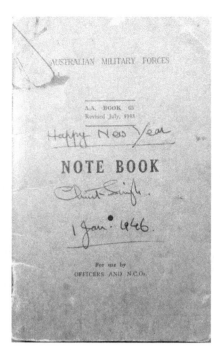

Chint Singh's diary

1½/46. Said good bye to 1945ᵗʰ which I suffered very much but again after 3½ years came into the light on 30th Sep of this year, at 2358 hrs 31st Sep. Dec. 1945 and Welcomed the Happy New Year of 1946 at ~~2358~~ 0001h. Jan: 1946 in the Mess of 19 A.O.D at cape Mom where in Sep. 1943 15 Indians had died in the Jap Hospital within ten days time. We sang very happy songs and had a rope trick. The I, Major Coll, Captain Steele and Capt. Steed visited their friend and said them Happy New Year. We ~~came~~ back at home about 0430. We had a nice day through out. In the ~~evening~~ I was invited in the Sisters Mess with Lt. Stone by Sister Kay Murch who had been very kind to me and my men since our release. She is very gentle, and very hospitable. She

A BRIEF SKETCH OF THE FATE OF 3000 INDIAN P.O.W. IN NEW GUINEA

WEWAK, NEW GUINEA: 4/11/45.   16 $\frac{5}{23}$ - 30 $\frac{5}{45}$

It was the most unlucky day for 3000 Indians who touched the soil of
New Guinea on 16th May 1943. We left Singapore on the 5th May 1943
in seven parties each consisting of about 600 - three of the parties
went to New Britain and the other four came to New Guinea.

The Japs had two cargo boats and we were kept in hell throughout the
journey. There was not enough space for us to sleep with our legs outstretched. Many of us contracted dysentery and no sanitary arrangements
were made for the patients. We requested several times that we be allowed to sit out in the cool breeze for a while but all was in vain.
We were not told where we were going or to where they were taking us.
One day we found our boat anchoring near a point and one of the crew
told me that the point was WEWAK and that we had to disembark there.
When we saw some buildings and the red roofed church on the hill, we
were a little pleased and thought that there would be some good roads
and a town.

When we came on to the road after unloading ours and the Japs cargo we
saw for the first time, black natives, with strange features, and we
were a little frightened of them. We had no knowledge that those ugly
looking faces would feed us and save our lives in the long run, and that
we would love them.

On the same day about 12 o'clock the Japs ordered us to carry our bundles and the Japs rations and marched us along the beach. When we did
not find any road; but on one side the sea and on the other swamps,
we were very much disheartened; but kept marching, still thinking that
there might be roads or a town further on. The guard themselves did
not know where to go. We passed three small streams by walking through

Chint Singh's personal account of his life as PoW

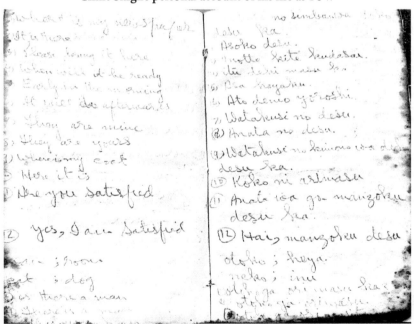

Chint Singh's diary - learning Japanese language

CHAPTER 2

LIFE AS A PRISONER OF WAR IN NEW GUINEA

IT WAS PERHAPS the unluckiest day for the 3000 Indians who landed at New Guinea on 16th May 1943. We left Singapore on 5th May 1943 in seven parties, each consisting of about 600 men – three of the parties went to New Britain and the other four came to New Guinea.

The Japanese had two cargo boats and we were kept in a dreadful condition throughout the journey. There was not enough space for us to sleep with our legs outstretched. Many of us contracted dysentery and no sanitary arrangements were made for the sick. We made several requests to be allowed to sit out in the cool breeze for a while, but it was all in vain. We were not told where we were going. One day we found our boat anchoring near a point and one of the crew told me the point was Wewak and we had to disembark there. When we saw some buildings and the red roofed church on the hill, we were a little pleased and thought there would be some good roads and a town.

When we came on to the road after unloading all the cargo, including the Japanese, we saw for the first time black natives, with strange features and we were a little frightened of them. We were not aware at the time that those ugly-looking faces would be the ones to feed us and save our lives in the long run and that we would come to love them.

On the same day, at about 12 o'clock, the Japanese ordered us to carry our bundles and the Japanese ration and marched us along the beach. We were very disheartened as there was no road. There was the sea on one side and swamps on the other. Despite this, we kept marching, hoping there might be roads or a town further ahead. The guards themselves did not know where to go. We passed three small streams by walking through them. The night set in and we were ordered to stop on the beach. During the night, we were again sent back to Wewak Point, a distance of about three miles, to bring the remaining goods. This was the worst day and night I had spent in my life. We were hungry and thirsty and kept marching throughout the night. Early in the morning we came back from Wewak having had very little sleep. It seemed as though the sea was also conspiring against us with the Japanese because while we were asleep the tide came up the beach and completely soaked our blankets and clothes. At sunrise, we marched on further and were ordered to make our huts in the swamps near Cape Wom. We used to walk to Wewak every morning at 0530 hours and return to our huts at 1830 hours in the evening. This continued for about two months and then we were ordered to make our huts about two miles from Wewak Point.

One day, we received orders: a Japanese colonel would inspect the Indian huts and the sick men. We were a little happy and thought he would listen to our grievances. Before his arrival, all the sick men were lined up. The colonel walked along the line and touched each man's forehead. The man whose head was hot was slapped on the face and sent to his hut, and the man whose head was cold was kicked and sent to the aerodrome to work. Most of the patients were suffering from beri-beri, dysentery and tropical ulcers and could not walk, and their heads were continually hot with malaria. Some of them would not reach the aerodrome before 3 or 4 o'clock in the afternoon, while others were severely beaten and left along the way. Those who went to the aerodrome returned to their huts by 10 or 11 o'clock at night.

After his inspection of the sick men, we had requested the Japanese colonel for the following:-

1. Humane treatment as laid down in international law.

2. Medicine and medical aid for the sick men.

3. Sick men should not be made to work.

4. Sufficient rations to keep ourselves fit – the ration being issued was not enough for two meals.

5. Fixed hours of work.

6. Cooks should not be taken to work but left behind to prepare a meal for the men when they came back.

7. Officers should not be taken to work, but should be treated as officers.

8. The punishment of beating and kicking should be stopped as no army in the world uses the punishment, nor is it written in any of the regulations.

9. Our medical staff should not be forced to work but should be left in the huts to look after the patients.

These were translated to him by an interpreter by the name of Fukai. The colonel listened and growled, "I do not know any international laws, so therefore, your requests cannot be granted. If you speak in this manner again, we will shoot you". We had shown him a copy of the international laws and told him it was signed by his government, but he threw it away. Then he lectured our guards and I came to know through the interpreter he told them that Indians work very slowly therefore beat and kick them.

On another occasion, we were informed their doctor would inspect the sick Indians. We were happy as we thought he would give them some medicine and treat them gently. To our greatest disappointment, the doctor carried out the same process as the colonel had. When we requested medicine, he replied they had no medicine for POWs. He informed us grass and leaves off the trees from the swamps would cure beri-beri. When we asked for something to dress the men suffering from tropical ulcers, whose wounds were getting worse and full of maggots, he replied if the ulcers were bathed in salt water, they would be cured.

It was 17th August 1943 when we were working on the Wewak aerodrome at about 0930 hours there was a sudden attack by Allied dive bombers. This was the first time we saw bombers flying so low and hitting the Japanese planes one by one. There were about 200 planes on the ground and not a single one was left capable of flying. We lost about ten of our men and an equal number were wounded. After the raid was over, we saw the Japanese turn very pale and they became frightened. In the evening I saw they were burning the Japanese dead in big heaps. Colonel Thakana arrived and asked the Japanese whether any of the Indians had died or not. When he was informed about the casualties, he was very surprised and said, "that is not a big number, more should have died". He then put the wounded men in a truck and brought them to our huts. When he reached the huts, he stopped the truck and we offloaded our wounded, who were crying with pain. The colonel got off the truck and with his hands started throwing dust on the wounded men, saying that was the medical treatment they deserved. Our doctors dressed them and did everything in their power to help, but without medical aid and enough food, the wounded men died shortly afterwards.

After this incident, during the night, the Japanese used to bring in their cargo boats and we had to unload them before sunrise. There was no time to sleep or rest, but we used to slip away in small groups for some time, turn by turn. There was also time for us to steal their supplies to make up for the poor rations issued to us by the Japanese.

Some of our men used to do two trips during the night and carry as much stolen rations as they could.

One day our huts were searched by the guard and they found about forty bags of rice and other stolen foodstuff. The guard called all the Indian officers and beat them severely and threatened them with the death penalty if it occurred again. There were only two courses of action for us to take - to steal and live and risk being shot by the Japanese or to die of hunger. We preferred the first, so we organised our men in regular parties for stealing rations and medicine. We used to keep the stolen rations in the swamps where the Japanese could not go and during the night we used to bring it in to cook and eat. Some of the rations we used to bury under the ground in tins. Many of our men were shot and many were severely punished with corporal or religious punishments, such as burning the beards of Sikhs, cutting the sacred hair of the Hindus and burning our religious books. Yet, none of these punishments could stop us. We had to steal to keep ourselves alive and this was the only way we could live.

The rations issued by the Japanese were never enough for more than two meals and moreover, it was so poor that within the first two months, we had about 200 cases of beri-beri. One day a Formosan workman came with a bundle of food under his arm. I asked him what he had with him. He showed me some sugar and demanded a pair of shorts in return, to which I agreed, as I hadn't had sugar for a long time. I told him of our ration difficulties, and he showed some sympathy and told me we should steal from the Japanese supplies, otherwise we would die of starvation. He also told me the Japanese would not give anything to anybody, so the only alternative was to steal.

His words stuck in my mind and I discussed this with our senior officer Captain Nirpal Chand[7]. He also agreed we should steal, so we organised groups and began our campaign to obtain extra rations. Our

7   2nd-Lt (Ty Capt) Nirpal Chand, 6/14 Punjab Regiment, Indian Emergency Commission 15th June 1941. He died on 22nd April 1944 and is commemorated on the Singapore Memorial.

ways of stealing became so crafty that we used to rob the trucks while going from one place to another. We also stole from the Japanese walking along the road with ration on their backs. Many times, when there was an air alarm, the Japanese used to run away leaving behind the dixies of cooked rice and vegetables. We used to eat out of them with satisfaction. There were certain men among our Japanese guard who used to send our men to steal cigarettes, sugar and milk and they used to take a share of the stolen articles. Sergeant Tekai, Corporal Hanada, Private Yasusak, Habeano and Tukura were the men of our guard who used to send our men to steal. Later, when the ration problem became more difficult, Lieutenant Mitsuba also joined the group. Sergeant Tekai used to select the strong men from among us and send them to the supply stores and sometimes used to accompany them. Once when Lance-Naik Bawa Singh and Sepoy Piara did not give the Japanese their share from the stolen food, they were tied to a tree, severely beaten, and later shot by Japanese.

From October 1943 onwards, the bombing became so terrible that the Japanese used to run two or three miles away from the beach and come back in the afternoon as the time of the bombings was always 8 o'clock until 11 o'clock in the morning. One day, it was about 0930 hours that one double bodied aeroplane (American Lightning) engaged about 10 Japanese fighters over Muschu Island. I was enjoying the tactics played by the American fighter and suddenly it fired a long burst and I saw two Japanese fighters catch fire and come down in the sea. The others ran away. One of the Japanese pilots parachuted and dropped into the water. I could see the pilot for about 30 minutes, but no Japanese boat went to rescue him. I said to Lieutenant Izumi, our guard commander, "You have got no regards for your men. Look, there is a pilot fighting for your country and he is trying to save his life, but you people do not care for him. If that pilot was ours and we were in the same position as you with all the facilities to save him, we would have sent as many boats as possible to rescue him." He replied, "The brains of our commanders have turned mad."

By the end of March 1944, the Wewak area and aerodrome were cleared. One could see only one or two Japanese aeroplanes coming in the afternoon from Hollandia and going back a few hours later. The anti-aircraft and other guns could be seen without their crews, while the Japanese were scolding those who had run away, leaving their guns behind. There were few drums of rice, fish and dried vegetables and in the evening one could see many Japanese stealing from one side and Indians the other. It gave me great pleasure when, one evening while I was with my stealing party, I saw there was a case of tinned fish – the Japanese and the Indians rushed to take it at the same time. There were about ten Japanese and six Indians. The Indians pushed them away and knocked them on the ground, took the box and made their way through the swamp to their huts. The Japanese kept watching like owls but could not chase the Indians.

Colonel Thakana ordered our guard to teach the Indians the Japanese language and drill. The programme was laid out – one hour before our march to fatigue and one hour when we came back in the evening. We objected and told them our brains were not good enough to learn the language and drill, but the guard insisted on it. We held a little conference amongst ourselves and decided not to learn, so when the Japanese gave the order for 'left turn', some of us would turn right and others would about turn. When they ordered us and taught us counting, we used to say one, four, seven and so on. In one month of training, we could not count to ten in Japanese. We were severely beaten, especially the officers. The Japanese used to say, "Your officers no good. Your head, fool." The guards were very tired of us, so they sent a report to Colonel Thakana, who became very annoyed with the guard and beat the Japanese officers, saying that their method of teaching was not good. Then the guard made big charts and painted them with different colours, but all these had no meaning to us. Colonel Thakana used to send his adjutant with new charts and new proposals, but to no avail. In the end they became very tired of us and dispensed with the idea saying, "Indians fool, no head, very low race". In this way, after one month's

struggle we succeeded in our mission, and the Japanese, with their infe-
riority complex, never ordered us the two hours beating parade.

The bombing on the coast had become so intense that the Japanese
were frightened of an Allied landing. We heard rumours the Americans
had occupied Lae. It was during the month of March 1944 one night a
submarine shelled the coast. Our guard ordered us to run into the bush
as there would be a big fight on the coast with the Americans. We went
and hid in the bush and there rejoiced very much as we thought soon
we would be in a new world. We did not care even for the mosquitoes,
which used to come in large groups and feed on us. The hearts of the
guards sank, and they were no longer growling as before. We did not
know our happiness would turn on us and there would be something
worse in store for us. As the night vanished, with it vanished our hopes.
"The Americans did not land," the boys said with a bleeding heart.

The following morning, the same programme of beating, abuse and
torture started. On 9th April 1944, we received orders to be marched
to Hollandia, a distance of about three hundred miles. We had to
carry one month's rations for ourselves, plus the Japanese luggage. We
requested some arrangement should be made for a boat or some other
transport to carry the rations and the luggage, but they snorted in fury.
We told them no army in the world had marched like that and we
were weak and not in good enough health to stand up to the march.
We were threatened with shooting, which was a common reply from a
Japanese soldier. Up until now, we had lost about 100 men out of about
539 since our arrival at New Guinea. On 13th April 1944, 400 men
marched to Hollandia. Before the march we had a secret conference and
decided not to march beyond But, a distance of forty miles, but to slip
away in groups into the bush. We heard rumours the Americans had
occupied Hansa Bay, so we expected them in about a month's time. We
had one month's ration issued by the Japanese and about two months'
extra in our hidden stores.

On 13th April 1944, our march to Hollandia started. Our average
march a night was four miles (nobody marched on the beach during

the day on account of the intense bombing). The sick, suffering from malaria, dysentery and beri-beri, were left unattended by the Japanese along the way. We requested them to give the men some medical aid, but were told to let them die on the beach. So, with our sick men, we left five healthy men who pretended to be sick. Our scheme was success-fully carried out and on 21st April 1944, thirty-one men reached But. We were severely beaten on the way and the Japanese became very tired of us. On 21st April, Lieutenant Mitsuba and Lieutenant Imamura took our senior officer Captain Nirpal Chand into the bush and we never saw him again. He left us with encouraging words as usual, "Don't worry, there are good times ahead". Before he was taken into the bush he was told by Lieutenant Mitsuba, "Either you collect your men here or we shoot you as you have instigated them not to go to Hollandia". He was undeterred by these threats and was not afraid to lose his life. He gave a daring reply, "You make transport arrangements and give medi-cal aid to our sick. We have never marched like this and cannot march." His loss was irreparable to us. He had guided us through many dangers of life and used to encourage us during the bombings and shellings. He himself never took shelter, but used to watch the Americans bombing and fighting in the air. When he used to see the Japanese fighters burn-ing in the sky and crashing down into the sea, he used to cry out, "Look Chint Singh, two Japanese aircraft have caught fire and are falling into the sea." I would cautiously raise my head out of the hole and used to tremble but enjoy the sight. He could not resist his joy and would cry out again, "Look, the four-engine bombers have dropped twenty bombs on Wewak Point and thirty in the harbour". And then, "God has saved us from unloading the big ship. The planes have unloaded their bombs on her. See how the flames are sending their message to Tojo".

Captain Chand had fifteen years non-commissioned service in the Indian Army, fought on the North-West Frontier of India, in the desert campaign, in Malaya and Singapore. His father[8] was a pensioner captain, having fought in France and Mesopotamia in the Great War.

In October 1945, the Japanese admitted before the War Crimes Commission at Cape Wom Headquarters that they had killed Captain Chand because he instigated the men not to go to Hollandia and also refused to go himself. Lieutenant Mamura said, "We took him into the bush near But, made him lie on the ground facing upwards. I was sitting on his chest; Lieutenant Mitsuba was holding his arms while Lieutenant Murai passed his sword slowly through Chand's neck. He died a few minutes after and we buried him". In this manner, our brave leader sacrificed his life for his men.

Today I find myself lucky enough to see the criminals being tried and will also see them executed. I have given a little solace to my heart and have written to his father, wife and son explaining the executors of their dear one have been caught and will be executed. Their dear one died a glorious death, which will be described in military history and other books. I hoped this would ease their pain and grief, to know that the Australian officers had caught the criminals and would punish them.

---

8   Hony Capt Bijai Singh, *Sardar Bahadur,* OBI, from Kangra, India. Enlisted in the 91st Punjabis on 23rd February 1887 and was commissioned as a jemadar on 1st October 1898.

Chapter 3

DARK AND GLOOMY DAYS IN SWAMP AND JUNGLE

ON 22ND APRIL 1944, we heard artillery gun fire towards Aitape and we visualised that the landing had taken place. We were told by the Japanese since we were the Indians who refused to go to Singapore, they would take us back to Wewak. There we would be bombed by the Allies. We marched back to Wewak, this time very happy in our minds, but had no idea there would be something more serious in store for us.

We had passed our time counting the days and months since the heaviest American bombardment of 17th August 1943, hoping for our release, but our hopes were all in vain. Our miseries and troubles increased with time. We came back to Wewak and stayed nearly one mile from the beach in the jungle. Some of the Japanese used to take our parties to steal rations for them from their senior officers. They also used to give a little share to the men who stole for them. We lost some of our men while doing this. This crime has also been admitted by Private Yasusaka before the War Crimes Commission on 30th October 1945.

We marched through the swamps to Rainimbo, about 10 miles from Wewak. It was the month of June 1944. The Japanese refused to give us any rations and would not give us even salt. We were ordered to make sac-sac and eat it. The grass in the jungle was our vegetables and lizards, grasshoppers, snakes and mice were our vitamins. In the swamps of New Guinea you can see the sac-sac trees just as you can see the palm trees in India. We had to cut them, chop them, and pound them, soak it in water – the sac-sac (white substance) settles down at the bottom and the wooden parts float. In other words, you can call it the juice of the trees. It has no taste and is hard to eat. We lived on it for a year and two months.

The sac-sac we used to make was put before the guards and it was up to them whether they gave it for one or two meals. We had to work from morning starting at 5 o'clock until the evening and we used to steal sac-sac during the day and thus have our full meals.

At Rainimbo in the month of August, two Japanese privates, Ishiyama and Yasusaka, tied officer Risaldar Rashid Mohd.[9] and Lance-Dafadar Mashuq Ali of the 3rd Cavalry and shot them for having stolen a watch and a piece of gold from them. This incident has also been admitted by these two criminals before the War Crimes Commission at Cape Wom on 1st November 1945.

The natives of Rainimbo were very wild towards us and one day they beat two of our men to such an extent that one died the following morning and the other about a month later. Their little boys used to beat us and the Japanese made them our commanders while we were making sac-sac. They used to ridicule us in their presence.

At Rainimbo, in the months of July, August and September 1944, we suffered a lot at the hands of the Japanese, the natives and nature. The wild grass which we used as our vegetables could not last more than a month. The rains became so heavy that our huts could not bear

9   Rashid Mohammad Khan joined the Indian Army on 20th September 1932. He was commissioned as a jamadar on 1st June 1940 and promoted to the rank of risaldar on 1st April 1941. He is commemorated on the Singapore Memorial.

them, and we had to live in the mud and the damp. We could not cook our sac-sac as the fuel was always wet and the Japanese feared smoke would make them the target of aeroplanes.

One day, Private Yasusaka searched the hut of Jemadar Kitial Singh and found some pawpaw, so they tied him to a tree for two days, beat him with sticks and kicked him. The two other incidents relating to the shooting of Risaldar Rashid Mohd. and Lance-Dafadar Mashuq Ali of the 3rd Indian Cavalry and Havildar Waryam Singh and Lance-Havildar Hazara Singh of 2/12 Frontier Force Regiment increased our terror very much. The shooting and killing of about a hundred Indians at But and about eighty at Boiken made this period very hard for us. We were in fear of death by the Japanese and hope for the day of release by the Allied troops.

The problem of our rations, especially salt, was more acute. The Japanese supplies had run out. Our hidden stores of rations were also exhausted. Four men of our party were bayoneted to death while trying to escape. Secret prayers did not help. The thundering clouds at midnight used to wake us as if we were hearing the heavy artillery fire of the Allies firing at Wewak and Mandai. We were bursting with happiness. Each one of us, whether literate or illiterate, had some knowledge about Australia. In the middle of the night, you could hear in every hut, men talking about Australia. Even the patients on their deathbed (many of whom died in the morning) talked of buying leather suitcases and woollen clothing for the coming winter in the cities of Australia. The officers could be heard thinking of buying something more - gramophones, wireless sets and wristwatches. But in the morning, everything seemed an illusion. Every morning full of hope would turn into a day full of terror. The orders came to march to Maprik, but the midnight guns did not stop firing and our hopes were not shattered. The most terrible time in our life which lay ahead could not have been predicted by any one of us.

Two hundred and forty prisoners of war marched to the mouth of death on 29th September 1944. One hundred and forty-six were left behind at Rainimbo, at the mercy of God. They had nothing to eat and no medical aid. In all likelihood, the Japanese may have killed or eaten them, as was proved later on. There were about 500 packages of Japanese luggage and we used to carry it in stages of five miles, covering a distance of about 20 miles per day. It took us three months to reach the Sepik River after marching about 1500 miles. Only nineteen Indians out of those 240 prisoners reached the Sepik.

When we left Rainimbo on 29th September 1944, we had 15 days sac-sac and little salt to feed on. We were all bare footed and had nothing to protect ourselves from the rain and mosquitoes. We were driven along the Hawain River without any track or path. The Japanese had stolen rations and tried to keep themselves off the path so the higher formations may not take the rations.

On the first day of our march when we were loaded like pack animals, it rained heavily and the loads became heavier. The river was in flood and four men were swept away but were rescued. The night was spent in the mud and we suffered a lot from it, however we became used to it. On the third day, after we had moved from the first stop, we left behind four men who could not walk. We had to cross the river about 20 times a day for three weeks during our trip. The tropical ulcers, malaria and beri-beri increased in large numbers and in various stages of the march. Fifty men were left behind.

When we left the river, we came upon very high mountains. We had never climbed such mountains and with such loads. Our sac-sac had finished, and we suffered very much on account of starvation. The Japanese ordered our sick men to make sac-sac and the others they kept on using as pack animals. We used to steal a small quantity from bags of rice and salt every day.

In the month of November 1944, there were about 150 Indians left. We had made the packages lighter by stealing and also by throwing others in the water as we crossed the river. The bags were broken and weighed less, but our power of endurance had decreased, and the number of men had greatly reduced.

One day, early in the morning, near the village of Ain I, Corporal Tekai and Privates Hibano and Yasusaka took Sepoys Kirpa Ram and Harman Singh of 6/14 Punjab Regiment. They tied their hands behind their backs and started beating them. They then took them before Lieutenant Mitsuba, who kicked them, put them in a nearby river and shot them. They were killed because they had stolen a handful of rice and were carrying it in their pockets. Nursing-orderly Maida had caught them.

The following day, Corporal Hanada searched the hut of Jemadar Harnam Singh[10] of 6/14 Punjab Regiment and found a bottle of quinine. He tied him to a tree and all the Japanese guards started beating him with sticks and kicking him. He was then left tied to the tree throughout the night and in the heavy rain. In the morning, Lieutenant Mitsuba and Corporal Shimizu took him into the bush, where Lieutenant Mitsuba cut his head off with a sword. This execution had been admitted before the War Crimes Commission Board.

After a few days we reached Ain III where our sick men started making sac-sac. In this area there were two mango trees, the mangos being good to eat with the sac-sac, but the repercussion of doing so proved very costly as, in spite of this diet, it caused the men to have weak legs. One could see the men with their faces and bodies seemingly healthy, but their legs could not carry their weight. Many could not stand or even bring water for themselves. Only about 60 men could walk. Those who could walk about two miles and manage to steal bananas from the native gardens recovered as the bananas helped to keep the body fit.

Towards the end of November, we reached a place called Sinangu, where we made another fifteen days' rations of sac-sac. Many who were still lingering on with the party died at this place. The natives gave us much to eat and many who were weak grew strong again.

We left this place on 1st December 1944, leaving behind twelve

---

10   Killed on 9 October 1944 and is commemorated on the Singapore Memorial.

Indians who could not walk. One of them was Girdhari Lal of 2/12 Frontier Force Regiment, my school mate. He was a religious teacher with good knowledge. He used to encourage the men by relating old and chivalrous stories of Indian rulers and princes. He was a first-grade clerk in the regiment.

The next day, 2nd December 1944, Havildar Karam Singh of 2/12 Frontier Force Regiment revisited the camp to see a relative who was too weak to walk and who had been left at Sinangu. When Karam Singh joined us again at Pachan, he told us the men we had left behind had been shot by the Japanese. I had some knowledge of the Japanese who had stayed back on the day of the march and brought them before the War Crimes Commission. Corporal Shimizu, who was one of them, admitted that on orders from Lieutenant Mitsuba, he along with Privates Yasusaka and Tokura shot the Indians who were unable to walk with the party. This is enough proof of the fate of the sick Indians who could not march with the party and were left behind.

We reached Yawa on 15th December 1944 and from this place Captain Ishar Singh[11] with eleven other Indians, escaped. I did not hear of them again. One officer, Jemadar Lachhman Singh[12] and Lance-Havildar Angrezu Ram, escaped and were caught by natives who brought them back to the guard. They were beheaded by Lieutenant Mitsuba with his sword in the presence of all Indians. During this time, seven men of the 17th Indian POW working party, who had escaped, were caught by the natives and were shot by the Japanese. We were strictly prohibited by the Japanese to talk to the natives or get anything from them. The natives, in turn, were frightened of the Japanese, as they had killed many of the natives in the presence of

---

11   Listed by the Commonwealth War Graves Commission as having died in December 1944 presumably having suffered a similar fate as the rest of the men who were caught by the Japanese. Ishar Singh was the son of Sardar Hukam Singh and husband of Gian Kaur of Choke Jher Chak 81, Sheikhupura (now in Pakistan).

12   Killed 15th March 1944. Son of Santa Singh and Basant Kaur, and husband of Charan Kaur of Kadiana, Hosiarpur, India.

others to scare them. Captain Mohan Harishchandra Hanawar[13] of 5/14 Punjab Regiment was shot by the Japanese in this area. The natives used to give him plenty to eat. One day some fish, pork and vegetables were found on him by Lieutenant Nimuri who tied him up and killed him.

At Yawa, the sac-sac trees were very bad and the output of sac-sac was very small. Also, there were no gardens nearby from where we could steal. Many of the Indian POWs died on account of ulcers and starvation.

On 1st February 1945, we left for Yakano, a village about 12 miles south of Yawa. Four officers of the party Subedars Ishar Singh and Ganda Singh; and Jemadars Ran Singh and Bahadur Singh, who could not march with the party, were left behind and shot by Lieutenant Mitsuba and his party. After two days' march we reached Yakano. This was a very bad place and the problem of sac-sac was worse than at Yawa. There were about six Japanese of the road construction party, one of them a lieutenant. They were very weak but used to get some fish, pork and sac-sac from the natives. I had only one pair of long trousers which I gave to one of them and in return he gave me some fish and pork. One day I was very sad and had gone to the jungle to get some fuel for the Japanese. I sat under a big tree and many ideas came to my mind. I cursed my fate and abused all the Gods we worship in India. I wept bitterly and could not do anything. There were thick jungles and swamps all around the camp and we could not escape. Everything was against us. The trust in the natives was lost. The Japanese used to kill the escaped POWs in a very cruel manner.

There was darkness all around us. Life was a great burden. Many times, the idea of committing suicide came to mind, but the heart was not strong enough to do it. When tears flowed from my eyes, I had a little repose of mind and the cool breeze made me sleep.

---

13   Mohan Harishchandra Hanawar was part of the Indian Army Reserve of Officers and was commissioned on 1st August 1937. He was killed on 31st October 1944. He was the husband of Ratna Hanawar, of Matunga, Bombay (now Mumbai), India.

When I opened my eyes, I found a good-looking pair of natives standing nearby and they were naked. I stood up, bowed to them, and started chatting. The wife of the native was a very good woman. Both showed some sympathy for me, and when I requested for something to eat, the wife went at once to her house a mile away, advising her husband and me to wait. We kept talking until the wife returned with a large bundle in her arms. She opened the bundle and offered me two large pumpkins, fish, bananas, sac-sac and sac-sac cakes. I had a razor blade with me, which I gave to her in return, and it proved a valuable gift as she was very pleased indeed and told me she would come to the same spot every day with food for me. I remained at Yakano for three weeks and every day she used to give me something which kept my health in good condition. However, many of our boys suffered a lot at this place.

Our talk and thoughts were almost continually about food; food we had enjoyed in the past, food we craved as prisoners of war and food we intended to enjoy after our release. I remembered my mother who used to give me the best food possible and how I used to complain. My mother would say, "Look, dear boy, one day you will lament and remember how you used to discard your mother's offerings and were insolent". The memory of these words pierced my heart and I wept bitterly.

One day, an officer named Subedar Sukhor-Shan Singh said, "I have Rs.150 and I will give them to anybody who can offer me a cup of tea." We used to say to each other "I will invite you to some festival and serve you special dishes." Captain Gopal Das[14] who was a very jolly man and a doctor, used to jump in and say, "I will invite you all to the wedding of my daughter and serve you with sac-sac and lizard dishes."

To say many of our men stayed alive on mere hope is no exaggeration, but hope would sooner or later be expended, and they would

---

14   Died 1st December 1944. Son of Lachhman Das, M.B., B.S. (Lahore).

die saying two words, India and America. We could see American aircraft flying every day and had hopes the Americans would soon come and rescue us. Many of our boys, even on their death beds, used to ask me, "Sir, will the Americans come at the end of this month?" I would encourage them with high hopes, but at the end of the month, invariably it became the end of the lives of many of the men who were lingering on with hopes only. I had remembered a verse written by W.C. Bryant which read as follows:

The light of smiles shall fill again,

The lids that overflow with tears,

And the weary hours of woe and pain,

Are the promises of happier years

This verse was always in my mind and I used to console my heart again and again, renewing the hope in it.

The hope that glimmered in the eyes of the dying men was too much for me. I told them many times I was confident the Americans would come at the end of such-and-such month and they had to pull themselves together and grow strong.

CHAPTER 4
NATIVE SAVIOURS

THERE WERE MANY instances when men foresaw their own deaths. Sepoy Lahori Ram of 6/14 Punjab Regiment told us on 5th March 1945 that on 15th April 1945[15], either we would be released by the Americans or he would be released by death. The former did not come true and sadly when the day came, on the evening of 15th April, Lahori Ram passed away.

We left Yakano on the 18th February 1945 for the Sepik River. On our way, we halted at a place called Pagwi for one night. There I met some Indians of the 18th Indian POW working party. They were also very weak and had been ordered to leave the place on the following day with us. There were two sepoys of that party about 40 yards distant from the rest. During the night I went to the native village as usual. The natives of this village were very good and welcomed us. Many babies, women and men came around me offering me bananas, pork and fish. While I was there, a native boy came running and told

---

15   Date of death recorded by the Commonwealth War Graves Commission as 10th April 1945. Lahori Ram was the son of Hari Ram and Umer Devi, of Batala, Mirpur, Kashmir.

me "Captain, two Indians die, finis, Jap doctor masta givim needle". The other natives who were there realised what had happened and were deeply sorry. They told me the Japanese had not given them anything to eat for two months and had made the natives look after them. The Indians were very good, they told me, and they used to sew their torn clothes for them. I told them to take me to where the Indians were.

I accompanied them to a hut where I found two Indians lying unconscious on the ground, breathing as if they were going to die in a short time. I covered them with their blankets and requested if they die, to bury them the following morning. They were sorry as they said they had fed them for two months and they looked as though they would be all right.

On the following morning Medigama and one of his wives gave us some more cooked sac-sac, fish and bananas. I thanked him very much for his help and then we left the place and later reached the Sepik River. We were put in canoes which were paddled downstream. It was very hot that day, which made it difficult to sit in the canoes. The natives paddled for about five hours until the sun set behind the horizon. We got out of the canoes and the Japanese ordered us to carry all our cargo, including their own, to a small, dirty hut given to them by the natives. Within a few minutes, many natives gathered around us and started addressing me as captain. I am not sure where they got this information. As we were not allowed to talk to the natives, I did not pay any attention to them, but by certain signs I conveyed to them to wait until it was dark and the Japanese were asleep. One of the guards was very annoyed when the natives gave one of my men some fish and vegetables. The Japanese snatched the food from him and threatened the natives, who ran away saying "pig tasole", meaning the Japanese were just like pigs.

When it grew dark, I went into the village. The natives were anxiously waiting for me. Their 'marys' (wives) brought cooked sac-sac, fish, bananas and pork. I had my meal, to my greatest satisfaction.

I talked to them for a long time. They did not like the Japanese. They told me the Japanese had burned a native village, bayoneted the children, raped the girls and women and shot the men. Their way of expressing themselves was very touching to the heart. During our conversation, one boy of about eight years old jumped up and said, "Captain! Papa, mama, brother belonga me fella, Japan man killim die finis." (the Japanese had killed his father, mother and brother). "Jap no good, white masta good tomas" (Japanese are very bad but white people are very good). I told them not to worry and said "Lik Lik time behind, plenty white masta come, Japan man Buggar up finis. Balus belonga white masta strong tomas, Japan one time sip belonga Japan, algeta killim finish." (White people are coming very shortly, Japanese army has been defeated and the white man's aeroplanes are very strong. They have sunk all the Japanese ships and killed all the Japanese). They were very pleased to hear this. They told me they wanted to give all the Indians something to eat. I thanked them very much, then returned to my hut and sent my men one by one to the village. The natives fed them very well and also gave them something for the following day.

The next day, we again sailed in the canoes, spending another night on the Sepik. We met eight other Indians of the 18th Indian POW working party who were also going towards the south. Our guards did not allow us to talk with the other Indians. The natives of this place were also very good and I did the same as usual, went into their village and received a hearty welcome.

The third day in the canoes was very troublesome. The canoes were very small and water used to seep into them with the slightest movement of the body. The night too was not as good as the others. Our next stop was a place called Mumeri on the river Korosameri, which is a tributary of the Sepik. The natives here were pro-Japanese. They did not give us anything, even at our requests. One of our men stole some vegetables and the natives caught him and beat him severely, but we thanked them as they did not tell the Japanese.

The following morning there was great turmoil and I guessed some Japanese commander would be arriving.

The Japanese guard told us that a high-ranking Japanese captain was coming. We thought for our own sake the captain perhaps would consider our condition and instruct the guard in our favour. Within a short time, the captain arrived in a canoe. With him were two Japanese officers and three privates. The most attractive thing was a big, tall native with six red stripes on his right arm, armed with a pistol and dressed in Japanese uniform. The Japanese officer turned out to be a major-general as I noticed his rank pinned on the left breast of his shirt.

The natives of the village were all lined up, including the old and young men and women. There were eight pregnant women amongst them due to deliver in a couple of days. All those things were very, very strange and even now my mind and hands do not clarify what I am writing is really a fact and not a dream. The Japanese were also lined up, but the Indians were left sitting in the hut watching. I was a little anxious, so I stood outside of the hut hoping the Japanese officer would see me and ask me something or instruct the guard for our good. However, after inspecting the Japanese, he talked to them and I could understand he had told them the Japanese forces and aeroplanes were very busy in India. They had finished with China and had received orders from Japan to continue the fighting in New Guinea. Within a short time, many reinforcements would come. I smiled a little at his foolish speech, but those words had been sent by God in Japan to his sons in New Guinea. My smile was noticed by one Japanese guard named Lance-Corporal Issi. When the general dismissed them, he came straight towards me and signalled for me to come to him. I thought the Japanese general might have instructed something good which I did not understand, but when I went to him, he gave me four slaps across the face and told me I was a bloody fool for smiling at him. I went back and sat down quietly. After that, the Japanese general and the big native captain turned towards the natives. According to the instructions of the Japanese officer, the natives were told to help the Japanese and supply them with food and fish. He then dismissed them, turned towards us, ignored us and went into his house.

It is interesting to add by this time, February 1945, there were only two Indians in the 26th Indian POW working party, none in the 16th and 17th party, eight in the 18th party, and nineteen, including myself, in the 19th party. The place was very unhealthy, and our hut was in the swamp and jungle, which was infested with brown-coloured mosquitoes – the blood suckers. These mosquitoes do not carry the germs of malaria but they suck blood at any time, whether day or night, one could see them swarming around in hundreds. We suffered because of these mosquitos at this place. We had no mosquito nets and not enough clothes to cover our bodies. Our ration was very poor in both quantity and quality and could not make up for the deficiency of blood sucked by the mosquitoes. As a result of this, we suffered from acute beri-beri.

Private Maida (the Japanese nursing-orderly) was suffering from dysentery and his boots became dirty with his uncontrollable motion. He ordered one of our officers, Jemadar Katial Singh[16] to clean his boots. The officer cleaned the boots but did not carefully examine them and a little dirt remained. Private Maida took a big stick and mercilessly beat the officer over the head. Katial Singh became unconscious, but the Japanese did not stop beating him. His head started bleeding and the blood flowed over his face and shirt. Katial Singh remained very ill for over one month and then died.

One day we were making sac-sac and Lieutenant Murai came to us. We were weak, so we were not working as quickly as strong men would. Lieutenant Murai called me and compared our work with the work of the natives. He said, "You India work no good. Slowly, slowly. Kanakas work very good, hurry."

---

16   Jemadar Katial Singh, 6/14 Punjab Regiment died on 8th March 1945. He was the son of Mehnga and Jamna and husband of Durgi of Batala, Mirpur Chowk, Kashmir.

I replied "Sir, Kanakas plenty kai-kai, pig, fish, sac-sac, plenty strong. India no strong, plenty malaria, no pig meat, no fish, no salt and no vegetable for kai-kai." The ugly looking face of Lieutenant Murai became even more ugly and he picked up a piece of wood about 4 feet long and 4 inches in diameter. He struck it hard at my head, but I moved a little and it caught my shoulder. I once again came to attention and bowed four or five times and apologised for what I had said. He was not satisfied with this so ordered the guard not to give even a small amount of sac-sac to me. The effect of this was that we stole double the quantity.

Our sick men used to work in the gardens while the others used to make sac-sac every day. The Japanese promised us that if we worked hard on the gardens, then they would give us some vegetables from it, but when the gardens flourished, they did not give us anything. Their formula was "plenty work, plenty kai-kai. India plenty work, no kai-kai." I have not been able to understand this formula until now. We worked sometimes continuously for five or six days for 18 hours every day. We worked in the scorching heat of the tropics, carried their loads like pack animals through the swamps and jungles, climbed mountains 3,700 feet high, but the Japanese were never satisfied. Three thousand Indians died due to the brutality of the Japanese. Was it not a deliberate cruelty to the Indians? There was nothing we could do in retaliation. Striking the guard or even talking back to them meant almost certain beatings. The only things we could do was to steal and sabotage, which we did. When the gardens were ready and the Japanese refused to give us any pumpkin from them, we would not let any pumpkin grow but would pluck the flowers. Hence, the Japanese too went without them. They used to say amongst themselves that the birds must have eaten them.

One day, Lieutenant Murai caught Sepoy Ram Singh of 6/14 Punjab Regiment with four lemons in his possession. He tied him to a tree and then the whole guard, in turn, started beating him. They beat him all day and night until he became unconscious. The following day, he was untied and put in the sun. In the morning, the Japanese ordered us to dig a grave for the man, which we did. Sergeant Kibbe, Lance-Corporal Iga Rashi, Private Tokura and Lieutenant Murai took him to the grave. Lance-Corporal Iga Rashi and Private Tokura bayonetted and buried him.

I made friends with one native named Buist. He was a cook for the padre who used to live at Karkar. He used to give me fish, pork, and sometimes vegetables and coconuts. I told him of my plan to escape and asked for help. He agreed to it but explained there was no track out of the village and there were jungle and swamps all around it. It was just like an island in a swamp and the only means of communication was by canoe.

The date and time for the escape was fixed for the night of 13th June 1945. We had a little store of sac-sac and had cooked enough for about four days' ration. We were ready and waiting, but Buist did not come until the morning. Consequently, we were very disappointed. I met him the following day and he told me the natives of Mumeri had run away to the jungle from fear of the Japanese. Some Japanese and the natives of Sangriman who were pro-Japanese, had chased them and it was dangerous to pass that way. Besides this, Buist too was very frightened by the Japanese, as they had recently bayoneted five natives. He told me to wait for some time and so we withheld our plan. Without him, we could not get out of the swamp as we had no knowledge of the country.

Chapter 5
LAST DAYS AS PRISONER OF WAR

THE JAPANESE MADE about two hundred hooks for catching fish. They used to throw them into the river on lines in the evening and in the morning, they would collect fish from them. I used to slip away after midnight, search the hooks and steal the fish. Many nights were a success. I had also stolen some of the hooks. I used to throw them in on a line and copy the process.

One day, I saw two Japanese soldiers halting on their way to Barmori near Karkar. One, a sergeant, was picking lice from his shirt and eating them. I asked him why he was doing this, and he told me he was suffering from beri-beri and as lice contained vitamin B, it would help him to recover from the disease. These Japanese soldiers were from some road construction unit. I was very surprised by the sergeant's actions.

One day I requested Lieutenant Murai to give us some of the medicine they had for beri-beri, but he told me to go away and eat red ants and grass. Only once a week did the Japanese allow one man to go and collect grass we could cook to eat as vegetables.

Once, Warrant-Officer Adachi, one of our guards who was suffering from dysentery, had soiled his bed, body and clothes with his uncontrollable motions. None of the Japanese soldiers cared for him, so he ordered us to clean him and look after him. He was in charge of the gardens where we used to work, and in the absence of others, used to eat the pumpkin and bananas. One day, he stole a pumpkin, cooked it and ate it in the jungle. This was the cause of his dysentery. On the same day, Sergeant Takashi went into the gardens but could not find the pumpkin. He enquired about the missing pumpkin from Adachi, who told him the Indians had stolen it. Takashi made us fall in and started beating us. We had seen Adachi take the pumpkin. However, we preferred to take the beating. If we had complained, Adachi would have beaten us more. In August, the Japanese took us to Kuvenmas, a distance of about 10 miles from Karkar. We were employed here to work only on the garden. The natives used to make sac-sac and give it to the Japanese who would ration it out to us. Before the war, there had been a hospital and a mission at this place. There is a big lake near the village where flying boats used to land. The people of this place loved the white man but had a great hatred for the Japanese.

This was the only place where the natives compelled the Japanese to catch fish and grow vegetables. They never gave the Japanese any pork. One day a Japanese named Lance-Corporal Agarahsi stole some sugarcane and sweet potatoes from the natives' garden. He was caught by the natives who took him before Captain Izumi. Captain Izumi and Sergeant Takashi called the whole village together and lined them up. Takashi got a rope and threatened the natives, telling them they could not call a Japanese soldier a thief. Everything belonged to the Japanese and the Japanese had all rights to take anything from the village. He caught the native who had referred to the Japanese as thieves, but at the request of all the other natives, he was set free. The natives were told, in the future, if they referred to the Japanese as thieves, they would be killed.

After this, the natives became more anti-Japanese, and this was very good for us. They started giving us four sticks of sugarcane and some vegetables every day. It helped us a lot and as a result our health improved.

The nature, natives and the place itself turned in our favour and after a few days, even the Japanese treatment changed. We were surprised to see this change in the Japanese mood. We concluded either good times were ahead or the Japanese would kill us after one or two days of good treatment because we had heard of such stories of Japanese butchery. The Japanese divided us ten Indians into three separate parties and sent us to different places and our suspicions became stronger. I tried to communicate with the other parties in order to plan an escape.

It was 16th September 1945, about 9 o'clock at night, when one Japanese soldier came and instructed our guard to take us to their headquarters. They ordered us to get ready at once, so we took our sac-sac and blanket and started.

The natives of this village were very sorry to see us go, especially one, Ribantua, as they had suspicions the Japanese would kill us. They had heard many stories of this nature. A few days ago, Ribantua had advised us not to signal aircraft (a thing which I had done in his presence three or four times, without success) as the Japanese had killed seven Indians at Sangriman. They had signalled the aircraft and were seen by the natives, who handed them over to the Japanese. It was due to this information I have now caught Major Kudo, commanding officer of that area, and brought him before the War Crimes Commission. He had admitted he had given orders to two captains of his staff to kill Subedar Rasil Singh[17], Jemadar Piara Singh[18], Havildar-Major Sant Ram, Sepoys Ram and Ganga Ram of 3/17 Dogra Regiment. He admitted they had signalled the aircraft and were working as spies.

---

17   Rasil Singh entered service on 22nd December 1919. He was commissioned on 1st December 1936. He died on 25th September 1945. He was the son of Pohlo Ram and husband of Janki, of Janauri, Hoshiarpur, India.

18   Piara Singh entered service on 11th September 1926. He was commissioned on 1st December 1941. He died on 20th September 1945. He was the son of Damodar and Jasodhan; and husband of Rasal Devi, of Haldra, Kangra, India.

Ribantua followed us and we reached the headquarters. It was early in the morning of 17th September 1945. A Japanese sergeant with papers in his hands appeared. He was the chief clerk in Ajor Kudo's department. He told us the Japanese government wanted to send information to our homes, so he took our home addresses and wrote them on two papers. We bowed to him and thanked him for his kindness. We concluded one of the following would happen - they would kill us and before killing us, wanted our addresses for their records; they had been forced by the Allies to send information with regards to Indian POWs to India; or the Japanese had surrendered and had been ordered by the Allies to submit returns about Indian POWs.

We thought about this over and over again but could not arrive at any conclusion, and these thoughts troubled us immensely. As John Milton had said, "Never can true reconcilement grow where wounds of deadly hate have pierced so deep". The Japanese must admit now they are universally hated and feared through their own savagery, arrogance, cannibalism, immorality and inability to protect the innocent, as even the most primitive natives of New Guinea had run away from their approach. The Japanese have lost their face on earth.

On the following day, a native who had been in another village came to me very excited and happy and told me "Pite Pinish. Big captain one-time olgeta Jap soldier go pinish. White masta Wewak stop." He was very happy and made us happy too, but we could not indicate our happiness as the pressure of the Japanese was still on us. After a few hours the officer commanding the guard ordered us to fall in and then addressed us saying: "The Japanese government has stopped fighting, our king does not want to fight any more. Tomorrow we will take you to Wewak, from where you will be sent to India. But mind you, you are still in our hands and are not allowed to talk to the natives." After this he walked off and we started working as usual - cleaning the dishes, washing the clothes, fetching the water, bringing fuel and so on.

In the evening, the natives called us to their "Mararo house" one by one and entertained us (a Mararo house was a central place for singing songs and entertainment. In all villages, one could find Mararo houses. They varied in size according to population. Generally, they were double storey houses). Their marys (wives) offered us meat, fresh fish, sticks of sugarcane and sac-sac for the journey the following day. I thanked them and promised to reward them for their help. (Lieutenant F.O. Monk recently promised me he himself would go to the village and reward these people with some good prizes.)

The next day we, the only survivors from a total of 539 of the 19th Working Party, got into canoes and paddled towards the Sepik river. All the inhabitants of the village came to say goodbye to us and as a result of their love, I could not check myself, so waved my hand and bid them goodbye. In response, all of them waved their hands, even the little babies, and shouted goodbye. Lieutenant Murai turned his ugly face towards me but did not have the courage to say anything. At this hour, the secret of our relationship with the natives was disclosed to the Japanese, but it was too late. As I learnt later, the sergeant who had taken our addresses had submitted the nominal rolls to the Australian forces.

In the evening we reached Sangriman where we met the only two survivors of the 18th Working Party whose original strength was 565. They were Havildar-Major Munshi Ram and Lance-Havildar Dina Nath. We discussed all that had happened to us and in the morning started again in the canoes.

After two days' journey we reached Tambanum, the largest native village on the Sepik. Here we met Jemadar Abdul Latif and Sepoy Abrahim, the only two survivors of the 26th Working Party, whose original strength was 309. Sepoy Jogindar Singh was the only survivor of the 16th Working Party, whose original strength had been 560. I met the guard of the 17th Working Party and they told me not one Indian of that party was alive. The party's original strength was 500 men. Thus, on 16th September 1945, we were the only 13 left out of about 3000 Indians who had not been accounted for at the declaration of peace.

At Tambanum was the headquarters of Major-General Shoge, commanding officer of the Sepik Force. He had recently left for Kararau on the Sepik. One of his staff officers, who was a lieutenant-colonel, came and addressed us with the following "We are now friends, war finish. You will go to India, but do not tell bad things of the Japanese armies to Australians and Indians." He then ordered Lieutenant Murai and three other Japanese to take us to Marienberg and hand us over to the Australians. On 25th September we reached Marienberg and were feeling very excited about meeting the Australians, but to our greatest disappointment, there were no Australians there.

One native came to me and gave me a leaflet dropped by the planes. We read the leaflet and it gave us great satisfaction to know the Japanese had lost the war and we were naturally very pleased indeed. Lieutenant Murai, however, became very sad and disappointed. To us, the world had been in darkness and we had no knowledge that Germany too, had surrendered. We had only been guessing until now and were finding out that our guesses had been correct.

CHAPTER 6

THE RESCUERS: AUSTRALIAN DEFENCE FORCES

IT WAS MIDNIGHT of 16-17th September. All thirteen of us in captivity had fever. We heard the voice of the Sergeant Takashi. He was much crueller than the grim, dark night itself.

Although the war was over, we, the prisoners, did not know anything about what was actually happening in the world. We were passing time as if there would be no liberation from this hell. Apart from that, the news we received from our local friend named Ribantua, was disheartening. The crime committed by three Indian soldiers was they had signalled the Australian planes for help. Nobody can surpass the Japanese in beheading unarmed men mercilessly.

We were kept as captives in bush huts made on the bank of the Kuvenmas Lake, the source of the Black Water River. We felt our end was nearing when we heard the voice of Takashi in that dreadful night. He ordered me to come with him, as I was the only senior officer amongst the survivors. All my men started staring at me. Without a word, I followed the Japanese officer as it was impossible to go against his order. Another two Japanese joined us when we reached the bank of the river. When we sat in the small boat and began heading towards the Black Water River, I started performing the *Gayatri Japa* in order to control my troubled state of mind and remain calm. In my experience, the *Japa* of *Gayatri* or *Bhagavad Gita* gave me peace of mind.

Our boat reached Karkar just past midnight. We went to the office of the Japanese officer, Captain Izumi, who was the supreme guard commander in charge of us. Along with him were another two Japanese officers. All had their pistols within their arm's reach. On the table, opposite the captain, were two pieces of fish baked in a mess tin. Izumi asked with a smile to eat the fish. Having not thought of any baked food for many days, my mouth watered, but a doubt came over me for a moment and I wondered why I was at the receiving end of this unexpected politeness now. I thought to myself, "perhaps they wanted to give good food just before they kill me". But I ate the fish as any more delay may have resulted in punishment. Afterwards, Captain Izumi started praising Indian POWs. I felt there must be some ulterior motive behind his behaviour as we never heard anything good about us from a single Japanese, even by mistake, throughout the three and a half years as POWs.

"Was there any difficulty faced by the Indian prisoners from the Japanese in all these days?" Izumi asked. "Not here. Japanese soldiers are very good. There was no difficulty at all from them." I replied reluctantly.

They also knew I was telling a lie. All the Japanese who were there knew this. But in that moment, all such things were inevitable. The Japanese had killed all my fellow men. Even normal rations had not been issued to the prisoners for almost 15 months now, including sugar and salt. As a result, many men died of hunger. It was the tribal people who came to our rescue when we were suffering. I have never seen such opened-hearted and friendly people in all my life. In spite of their fear of the Japanese, many local men went out of their way to help us and not only that, they used to teach us how to eat, what to eat and what not to eat. For example, they told us about the vegetables and different kinds of potatoes grown in the jungles and about snakes, frogs and insects, etc. Some of us even discovered how to overcome calcium deficiency by eating the ashes of the bones thrown by the Japanese.

With my statement, it seems Captain Izumi felt happy. He said enthusiastically "Japanese and Indians have been friends in the past and will remain friends forever." He said that he had called me to break the good news and said, "Our Emperor has decided to end war with Americans. Accordingly, it is ordered that you will be freed and sent back to your country and immediately you all will be sent to Wewak port with that intention."

"We are obliged sir," I said, "I can never forget you." And I left the room. Takashi brought me back to the barracks in the same boat. All my friends felt happy when I shared this news with them.

Next day, the Japanese officers subjected us to a severe interrogation. When answering them, we had to be very careful. There was no guarantee until their promise was put into action that we would be freed and sent back to our homeland.

On 28th September, the thirteen of us were brought in a steamer to Marienberg. Even at this stage, the Japanese were not ready to accept their defeat in the war. Before we arrived at Marienberg, another two lost their lives. Sepoys Jai Ram and Abrahim died at an interval of half an hour. They died happily. Early in the morning Sepoy Jai Ram told me, "Sir, I know I will not see India and the new world, but I am happy now to know we are no longer prisoners of war. I think I am like a free man and will die like a free man and my soul shall be free. I am not dying as the other Indians have died by breathing their last breath under Japanese pressure. Their souls will not find any rest, but I am confident I am dying a peaceful death and it is enough for me. I wish that you all go safely home and see your families. When you reach home, see my parents and tell them Jai Ram died a peaceful death and there is no need for them to worry." One and a half hours later, Jai Ram departed from us forever. Jai Ram and Abrahim sleep a heavy sleep at Marienberg on the bank of the Sepik River, quite calm and in repose.

Just after we finished their burials, there came a prominent turning point in our life which has been expressed in the following entry which I wrote on 4th October 1945 at Angoram:

We are reborn at Angoram on 30th September 1945. It was the loveliest Sunday of 30th September 1945, when I was sitting in a native hut at Marienberg on the left bank of the Sepik River. Suddenly, a Japanese boat buzzed and stopped in front of the hut. A soldier came with a letter in his hand and asked for the Indian officer. I went forward, took the letter, opened it and it read as follows:

ANGORAM

29th Sept. 1945

To O.C. Indian Troops,

Marienberg.

I am sorry that I was not at Angoram when you called two days ago. I would like you to bring your Indian soldiers back to Angoram in the Japanese boat. We have a doctor here and plenty of good food. A boat from Wewak will call here at Angoram on Thursday or Friday and will take you to Wewak.

(Sgd) F.O.Monk

O.C. Angoram.

Apart from that, the Japanese officer who brought that letter also said all the Japanese should surrender themselves. It was the letter which rescued us from the oblivion of darkness into the new and happy world and changed the whole course of our lives. The sympathetic and kind words served as a hundred doses of Vitamin B to us who suffered from beri-beri. The soldiers started singing and forgot the miseries they had suffered, while the hearts of the Japanese standing guard over us sank. The faces of the guard turned pale when I told them we had been called to Angoram by the Australian commander. After saluting our two dead, who unfortunately breathed their last breath in the early morning at an interval of half an hour, we left the place.

(On hearing the report of the arrival of Indian POWs, Lieutenant Monk recalls when he went down to see them "...it was heart-wrenching. Ten of these poor fellows were lined up in two ranks. Some were sitting because of the sores on their feet or their condition generally was such that they could not stand, but all were rigidly at attention despite their rags and their pitiable condition. In charge was a smart-looking man, Jemadar Chint Singh, also in rags but with the most military bearing, who marched up, saluted and said 'Sir, one officer, two NCOs and eight other ranks reporting for whatever duty the King and the Australian army requires of us'. I found it very hard to reply to him. I still feel much emotion when recalling it."[19])

---

19   F.O. Monk, Unpublished memoir, 1940-45. [MSS1184] Australian War Memorial.

Chapter 7
TIDE TURNED

AFTER THREE HOURS, the boat reached Angoram. Local boys were waiting for us at the river bank. They hurriedly cleared the cargo from the boat. A boy sent by Lieutenant Monk (officer-in-charge, Angoram) guided me to his bungalow. I found the three officers (Lieutenant Monk, the doctor and Warrant/Officer P.F. Feinberg) busy talking to Kanakas. They left their job, welcomed me and accompanied me to see the other Indians, who were anxiously waiting to meet their sympathisers. Out of great happiness, we had a little parade of three cheers to His Majesty, the King, Emperor of India, and the Allied Forces, who had saved us from the brutalities of the Japanese.

The commander inspected the men and spoke encouraging words to them. Then the three men began their job. The doctor attended to the serious cases and gave them proper medical aid. It was the treatment without which hundreds of POWs had died worse than a dog's death. The commander guided us to a newly built house and instructed the local boys to make new and comfortable beds and supply all the necessities. The commander and warrant/officer brought clothes, soap and other luxuries we had not seen for many years. The first thing, which each of us impatiently tasted, was salt, not used since July 1944. The three gentlemen remained busy supplying all available comforts. In the meantime, tea was ready and we had biscuits and tea to our greatest satisfaction. Suddenly one of the Indians remarked, "Sir, today we have been reborn at Angoram." True, as the soldier said, we had been out of existence for three and a half years. We did not know the world and the world knew nothing about us. Our temporary home had been in the swamps and jungles, and our food a little sago, grass and insects. We did not know of the greatest achievements won by the Allies and other happenings of the world. The only news communicated to us was the Japanese had reached New Delhi. For us, this world was nothing but hell, and for many years, we did not find anybody who could drag us from it. We were not allowed to write any letters home, nor to anyone else. We, pale and swollen, suffering from beri-beri, were tired of life and within a few months were going to join our dead.

We departed after having tea, to our satisfaction. We were still clad in the same clothes and had with us a blanket which had been issued in May 1943. We had a hot bath and were provided with new clothes. The three officers did not rest till our dinner was ready and everything neatly and satisfactorily arranged. The commander said, "I would be very glad to see you comfortable and eating good meals to your satisfaction." With these words, they departed and the night set in. We offered our prayers and sang songs of happiness after a long period of two-and-a-half years. In this way, our re-birth took place in this land of Angoram on 30th September 1945.

We were only eleven out of 3000 Indians who had disembarked at Wewak on 16th May 1943. Most died of beri-beri caused on account of insufficient food lacking both in quantity and quality. Others died because of improper medical aid, hard labour for days and nights, long marches with heavy baggage and unhygienic surroundings. Many deaths were mainly due to malaria, tropical ulcers, dysentery and bombings. Many were unfortunate to have been killed and eaten by the man-eaters of Japan. It makes me shudder when I recollect the worst period of our lives which no human being can imagine. There is a long tale to tell about this unknown period of my life.

Now we are getting better and putting on weight and are well looked after every day. The doctor attends to us four or five times a day and the commander looks after us and provides us with many comforts.

At Angoram, Lieutenant Monk supplied us with many newspapers and books, which introduced us to the new world. The world seemed very complicated from the time we had left it and it would take a lot longer than a few days or even weeks to understand and mix with it. Small things of no importance in daily life were a miracle to us. For example, the material used for dressing Jemadar Abdul Latif's foot (tropical ulcers) and other medical material, the different variety of foods, especially those in tins such as tomato juice, apricots, or curry powder. These were the highest of luxuries to us. The use of soap, toothpaste and shaving material was another added luxury. The use of oil in the latrines for cleansing also brought back memories of our life which we had foregone a long time ago.

We passed the happiest time in four years at Angoram until 12th October 1945. Our health improved tremendously and it was surprising to our well-wishers. None of us, with the exception of Sepoy Lakhu Ram, could walk continuously for more than 500 yards. We had to take a rest before marching further. Within these twelve days, we gained a lot of weight. I do not know how much, but it was astonishing.

On 12th October, early in the morning, two very nice-looking barges anchored on the Sepik near our hut. We enjoyed their presence as one might enjoy the latest picture from Hollywood. Everything on them was new to us, especially the crew. I was introduced to Major Fogarty, G.I. 6th Australian Division, and we were very pleased to meet each other. He told me about the Indian troops in the desert who fought side by side with his regiment. He had great admiration for them. He told me of many daring and enterprising deeds of the Gurkhas. He was very proud of them and in the latter part of his conversation, I learnt his brother-in-law was second in command in one of the Gurkha regiments. It gave me great pleasure when he told me how Subedar Lalbahadur Thapa of the 2nd Gurkhas won his Victoria Cross. He also told me in this war the Indian Army was at the top in winning the Victoria Cross. I was also pleased to hear that another 192 Indians had been recovered by the 6th Australian Division in New Guinea prior to the peace declaration. The total survivors then amounted to 203.

After this, Major Fogarty went ahead and ordered us to get into the barges and go to Wewak. We departed from our friends in a very sad state. Lieutenant Monk and the doctor were also very sad, as they loved us greatly. We felt as though we were departing from members of our family and so did they. We left the place, waving our handkerchiefs to them until we were out of sight.

We arrived at Marienberg again in the evening. There were about 500 Japanese under Australian guard waiting to go to Wewak in the barges. Here we found five Japanese of our guard, one of them being Warrant-Officer Adachi, about whom I have spoken before – and another Lance-Corporal Sakamoto. The latter would not allow me to relieve myself when I, with 30 other Indians, was put into a dysentery hut at But, on our march to Hollandia. There were four sentries standing over us at this hut and they did not allow us to sit or relieve ourselves. Anything and everything we did on our beds. This N.C.O. was the senior man at the time and that night was terribly spent. Our officer, Captain Nirpal Chand, was taken into the bush and killed while we were confined to our beds. The hut, which was already dirty, became even more unbearable and life was hard. We heard the guns firing towards Aitape and saw the Japanese running here and there like mad dogs. We had started counting the hours of our life.

Here at Marienberg, the tide of our life turned and my pet verse by W.C. Bryant proved true:

"The light of smiles shall fill again

The lids that overflow with tears

And the weary hours of woe and pain

Are promises of happier years."

Our worries and sorrows turned into happiness. At the moment one Indian verse by a famous poet came to my mind and I repeated it:

"Badshah ko chahe gadagar kar de tu,

Gadagar ko badshah kar de

Ishara tera kafi hai

Ghatape men aur barhane men."

(Oh Almighty father, you can make the king a beggar and the beggar a king. Your little signal is enough for the fall and the rise.)

Our men got the Japanese of our guard and ordered them to get fuel, clean utensils, light fires and get water for cooking our meals. They also checked them for bringing poor fuel and not washing the utensils properly, for which we had severe beatings for three and a half years. Our men became a little wild and repaid some of their scores.

There I also saw some Japanese of the local guard force who had warned me sixteen days ago not to talk to the natives. The commanding officer of the guard force, when he saw me, sent a man at once to get four chickens for us. He came and offered the chickens to me and bowed. I made him remember the day he warned me and then told him to go.

I had told our stories to Lieutenants Alex Galt and Keith W. Peterson, of 43 Landing Craft Company, who were in charge of the Japanese and they informed me we could use the Japanese. They had collected a huge dump of weapons and ammunition which the Japanese had dumped in the river. Lieutenant Peterson gave us some curry powder, so we prepared chicken curry and rice for dinner. It was the first time we had had chicken curry in three and a half years. We shared it with the Australians who were very much pleased to taste it.

After this, I interrogated Lance-Corporal Kiroka who was with Lieutenant Mitsuba when our four officers, who could not walk, were killed. He admitted to this in the presence of all the Australian soldiers who were very interested in our stories and who sympathised with us very much. They gave us every sort of comfort they could.

Here I saw a launch, M.L. No. 1347, very nicely painted. There were men with long beards on the quarterdeck. Sepoy Chain Singh, who was standing near me, asked, "Are those men POWs recovered by the Australians?" I gazed again and again and was inclined to agree with him. They were dressed in only short pants but had long beards the same as us. After a short time, one Sub-Lieutenant Wilkinson of the Royal Australian Navy came to me. He talked for a while and then guided us to the launch. He introduced me to one of those bearded men as the captain and the others as the crew of the boat. Here my guess failed, but the impression was still on my mind so I asked the captain, "Were you a POW sometime before?" He was a keen-witted man and replied, "I keep the beard to keep prestige over the crew and also to frighten the Japanese." His answer pleased me very much. He was only 24 years of age, thin, but strong, with a very cheerful and intelligent disposition. He was Lieutenant Marsden Hordern of the Royal Australian Naval Volunteer Reserve and came from Sydney.

Both of these gentlemen guided me to their cabin, which was very nicely decorated. I felt very comfortable. Everything in that wonderful place was strange to me. There was a refrigerator, radio set and many other comforts. I had a nice cool drink of squash, my favourite drink, the first since being taken into captivity. In the meantime, Lieutenants Galt and Peterson also joined us and I spent a very pleasant time in their company, too. They were very interested in knowing about our sad stories and I kept 'ear bashing' them until midnight. Lieutenant Hordern showed me some good photos and gave me very interesting novels to read. Then I slept on the quarter deck in a very nice and cosy bed. I thought myself very lucky to enjoy these cherished comforts again for which we had pined so long. In the meantime, the crew were very busy with entertaining the other Indians. They gave them new things to eat and (unlike the Japanese) stuffed them with bundles of chocolates, biscuits, milk and so many things. They all went happily to their barges. Lieutenant Hordern and I kept talking until late in the night. Many times, we said goodnight, but he was so keen he used to start again. However, I was overpowered by sleep on a comfortable bed and I fell asleep mid-sentence about which he reminded me in the morning.

On Saturday, 13th October 1945, I got up at about 8 o'clock and found the launch sailing towards the mouth of the Sepik River. I went down to the cabin and went into the dressing room, which was adjacent to it. I used the latrine but could not manage to figure out how to use the mechanical apparatus for disposing of the excreta. Lieutenant Hordern was watching me and came smiling and demonstrated its function. That was the first lesson I had in mechanics that morning. I was told I could use anything in the cabin at my discretion and make myself comfortable, which I did and found myself in an entirely new world. Then I had breakfast. Everything on the table was strange to me. When I put four teaspoons of sugar in my teacup, my hosts laughed and Lieutenant Hordern smilingly said, "Don't finish all our sugar, we have not got enough now." I had a very nice breakfast. After this, the second lesson in mechanics took place and I learned all about the new tommy gun and a few new pistols. This was followed by firing practice, logs in the river being the targets. I fired about 100 rounds.

At about 0930 hours, we left the river and began our sea voyage. The scenery was lovely, but I felt sea sick so I went down below to sleep. I woke up at 1600 hours and when I came up on the quarter-deck, I saw Dame Hill and its surroundings, which had sealed the fate of 3000 Indians when the Japanese cargo boat anchored at that very same place on 16th May 1943. The old memories again became fresh, but it was a change of atmosphere. When we had left the place in June

1944 and gone into the hills, it was almost a desert, but now it looked like a big city. There was a very big ship anchored next to us, taking many Australian troops home. There were many other boats which were new to us and we had never seen so many there before while we were unloading the Japanese cargo ships. The most surprising thing I saw was a 'Duck' sailing on the sea and driving on the beach and road. Then I saw the tiny little vehicles called jeeps running here and there – these too, were strange to me. We felt the world had advanced a great deal, and we really had spent the period of imprisonment worse than animals. Lieutenant Hordern signalled the Duck which came and we put Jemadar Abdul Latif on to it and sent him to hospital. He had not slept for the last two nights on account of much pain in his foot. Lieutenant Hordern got a jeep and we had a ride throughout the whole area where we had worked, received beatings and suffered all the brutalities of the Japanese. It was a very fresh memory. I saw Japanese trucks, barges and aeroplanes burnt and destroyed all over the place.

I went to Wewak Point and was very impressed to see the nice roads, fine buildings and bridges which had cropped up in such a short time compared to the Japanese who had built one bridge in one month using Indian labour. We came back on-board in the evening and had a nice dinner. When I sat on the quarterdeck of a friend's boat, I felt something else, which my diary of 13th October 1945 describes, "The Wewak area is just like Amritsar on Diwali day. The glittering of the lights on the sea is just like the scene from the Golden Temple of Darbar Sahib in the holy tank. It seems a very big city with the works of electricity. It reminds me of the Diwali festival, which I passed at Amritsar in the company of my wife, in October 1940. (Amritsar is the second biggest city in the Punjab near Lahore. It is worth seeing during the Diwali festival – which is one of the biggest festivals in India and which is celebrated throughout the country.) The interesting thing which charms is the decoration of cities, houses and temples with lights of different colours and shades. The Golden

Temple of Darbar Sahib in Amritsar is the most sacred place of the Sikhs and is highly decorated during this festival. It is respected by all castes and creeds for its splendid beauty. During the Diwali festival, the lights from the temple reflect on the holy tank and add to its beauty."

A hut built by Capt. Nirpal Chand and Chint Singh, destroyed by Allied bombing

View of Wewak harbour, where Chint Singh and his party
disembarked on 16th May 1943

The notorious drain of Colonel Thakana, full of mud,
hundreds were wounded and died working on it

Chint Singh taking salute after being rescued by Australian army

Chint Singh and his men, the survivors

Chint Singh with natives of PNG

Chapter 8
TIME FOR JUSTICE

I ENJOYED THE scenery very much, the value of which is known only to me. No one else in the area could find as much pleasure as I did. I slept on the quarterdeck for the second night and on the following morning we sailed for Muschu Island where 10,000 Japanese POWs were kept. On our way to Muschu, I saw the coast where we used to carry Japanese cargo and it had completely changed since we left it. Every tree, a bend on the beach and all minor things brought back past memories.

I went ashore at Muschu with Lieutenants Hordern and Peterson, and I was very surprised to see the Japanese nicely fed and well treated. There was a nice hospital and big dumps of food and clothing, but their hygiene conditions were the same as ever. There was filth all over the area. The Australians ordered them to keep the area clean and warned them for not doing so.

We met a Japanese captain who was a doctor. He did not pay any attention and did not pay us respect. I called him and asked him why he did not salute. Sepoy Chain Singh, who was with us, took a stick

got everything. Send it to Tojo as a victory gift." The Japanese doctors
were cruel to us than any other men.

General Adachi and party surrender to officers of 2/7th Battalion, Kiaravu, PNG,
11th September 1945 (AWM128799)

Many years later, Maredan Hordern recalled his meeting with Chint

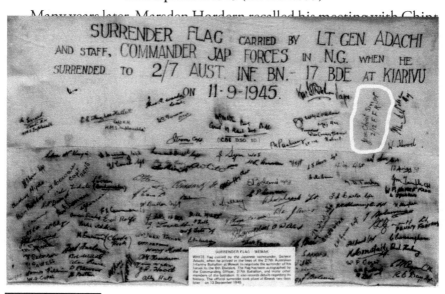

Chint Singh's signature on the surrender flag. (AWM135974)

20   M. Hordern, *A Merciful Journey, Recollections of a World War II Patrol Boat Man*, Victoria,
The Miegunyah Press, 2005, pp. 262-269.

dead… When you come to India here is my address, Jemadar Chint Singh, Village and Post Office Jalari, Via Naduan, District Kangra, the Punjab, India. My home will be yours. You have made me a happy man, and I will take you to the interesting places of India, and to the sacred places of my religion in which you have said you are interested. Goodbye, goodbye."

Chint Singh then came to attention, gave Hordern a Sandhurst salute and shook his hand. Hordern also makes mention of the incident when Chint Singh lost his temper at the insolence of a Japanese POW and assaulted him. He was unrepentant on being reprimanded. Hordern writes "he was content; after years of torture and cruel abuse, he had enjoyed his moment of revenge and got it off his chest."

We came on board again and I said goodbye to the Australian naval patrol boat M.L.1347. We sailed again from Muschu Island to Cape Wom. There I saw the swampy area where we had come for two months in 1943. The most important and everlasting memory is a mango tree on the beach. When we had no vegetables and no other food with which to eat our rice, then we used to get ripe mangoes from this tree, boil them and eat them with our rice. For us, this was far better than anything else on earth. The delicious and nourishing food of the Punjab, the tinned fruits and milk and butter from Australia, had no significance in our eyes. At that stage of adversity, when everything was hard on us, the mango tree did its best for us and fed us. On the beach, I met Major Calley of 6 Australian Division Headquarters who treated us very gently and arranged transport to take us to 2/15 Australian Field Ambulance. When we arrived at the hospital, we were given hospital clothes and nice, soft and comfortable beds.

Majors Geoffery Goding and Blair Widmer of the field ambulance came and examined us, prescribed medicines and gave instructions for special dishes. We received a very hearty welcome in the hospital. Major Calley arranged to send cables and letters to our families in

India. I wrote my first letter to my wife and brother since February 1942. It took me a long time to write and rewrite it as I could not understand what I was writing or what I should write.

In the officers' ward, I met Lieutenant Haydon, who was also a patient. He and other officers in the ward kept us happy. Lieutenant Haydon brought a chess set and we used to pass most of our time every day by playing chess. Every day, he used to do something for me and Abdul Latif. Major Widner gave us very good books to read and he was very interested in us. Every day he used to spend some of his precious time with us and had given the ward orderlies orders to keep us very comfortable.

In the men's ward, life was more pleasant. At any hour of the day, one could see four or five Australians sitting, talking and laughing with every individual Indian. Though the Indian soldiers could not speak or understand English, they were trained enough (by the Japanese who never gave orders in any other language but Japanese) to express their ideas which could be understood between them and there grew a great friendship among these men.

Sergeant Ron Bader was exceptionally kind to them. Hamir Singh, who could speak English, was the target of the ward. Sergeant Bader used to check everything and make sure the Indians had all that they wanted and were nicely treated. On many occasions, he worked as ward-orderly for them. He had a great and keen interest in them. The Indians were eating too much and an ordinary hospital meal was not sufficient, therefore special dishes were arranged and a drum of milk was put at their disposal every morning. Every day, each Indian would drink about five or six cups of milk. Sergeant Bader was so interested that he wrote letters to the Indian soldiers' families in India, telling them there was no need to worry as their sons were being well cared for. When they became a little better, Sergeant Ron Bader used to take them to the pictures in an ambulance. It was a very interesting time for both sides; but the Indians enjoyed it far better than anyone else. All these things were unforgettable to the Indians.

On 16th October 1945, we were visited by a nursing sister who took a keen interest in talking to us and consoling us and who was also very good to us. In the evening, blood transfusions were given to Lance-Naik Sher Singh and Sepoy Chain Singh. It was the first time I had ever seen blood being transfused. Both of them received two pints each and it improved their health very much. Their faces and appearance in general were quite different the following day.

War Crimes Investigation

On 18th October 1945, members of the War Crimes Commission came to see us. They were:

10. Major J. Lowry – 30th Australian Infantry Battalion

11. Captain D. Bruce – 30th Australian Infantry Battalion

12. Lieutenant C. G. Stone – 2/3rd Australian Infantry Battalion

I narrated the entire story of our imprisonment with a detailed account of murder and torture, which I had recorded on scraps of paper all the time in anticipation of our release[21]. Our sufferings and tortures at the hands of the Japanese were so horrible that one day I made an oath that if I remained alive, I would try to tell the world of their inhumanity. I gave similar instructions to my men. I used to tell them if I were to die, then they must take my notebook and take the first opportunity of relating the sad fate of the 3000 Indians. Today, I find myself very lucky the Almighty Father has fulfilled my wish and greatest ambition in life and I am putting a part of the story before you, the readers, and I sincerely hope that it was His wish to bestow upon me this duty which I have taken with great interest and pleasure.

A list of the other 191 Indians who were recovered by the Allied

---

21   "They, particularly, Chint Singh, were in great demand at Wewak for the War Crimes investigations. Chint had kept an extraordinary secret diary in tiny writing ever since their capture. It was written on the back of labels from Japanese food tins, on bamboo leaves and on anything else that would support writing." F.O. Monk, Unpublished memoir, 1940-45. [MSS1184] Australian War Memorial.

forces during the campaign in New Guinea was shown to me and I was very pleased to see some of my friends and relatives amongst them. They were taken to Australia and I could not see them. Now the total number of Indians recovered has amounted to 201 out of approximately 3000. I had hopes there may be some still in the jungles.

I was taken to the movie theatre by Lieutenant Hordern and it was the first film I had seen since January 1942. The newsreel was very interesting. I saw the surrender of General Yamashita – "Tiger of Malaya" (named by the Japanese) to the Allied forces in the Philippines. I also saw many dejected and demoralised Japanese POWs. In the pictures, I enjoyed the scene of a railway passing through the mountains and near waterfalls. It reminded me of my journey from Bombay to Poona in the electric train. It really was very exciting to me. The place where the picture was shown was near No. 3 Japanese harbour, which was once the filthiest area in the district but now was very nice and clean. "This is heaven", said my mind to me and once again old memories clashed with the new. I did not take as much interest in looking at the film as I did by looking at the surroundings and the different life led by the people of this world.

The most difficult task for us as POWs was to fill our stomach by hook or by crook. We did not care for any humiliations or for our lives. We ate the dirtiest things imaginable and the most wild things on earth. We used to find it a pleasure to eat in the same wooden and earthen pots as the natives, and to scratch something from the Japanese dixies. We never thought of boots or shoes or washing and cleaning our ragged shirts. Our lives day and night were spent trying to get anything we could to eat from anywhere, and thus live as long as one could hope for.

When I finished with my story, the War Crimes Commission 6th Australian Division issued an order for the capture of all the guards of the Indians, and then brought them from Muschu Island to Cape Wom, where they were kept in a barbed wire enclosure. In the evening, I was taken by Lieutenant Leslie Trout of the Engineers unit in his jeep to see a concert performed by the Royal Australian Air Force and it was very good.

On 19th October 1945, I was taken by Captain Bruce to 6th Divisional Headquarters to enquire and interrogate the cases. The president of the committee was Major Lowry and the members were Captain Bruce, Lieutenant Murray and Lieutenant Stone. The first man who was brought before us was Lieutenant Takesiko Tazaki of the 18th Japanese Army. This man had eaten an Australian soldier. After a long interrogation, he admitted an attack on Suain in July 1945. When he was weak and hungry, he ate the flesh of an Australian soldier so he could regain his strength to carry on. This was all translated by an American born Japanese interpreter.

Then came the turn of Lieutenant Hisaneo Mitsuba, one of the officers of my guard. I had accused him of the following charges:-

1. Killing Captain Nirpal Chand of 6/14th Punjab Regiment at But on 21st April 1944.

2. Killing Lance-Naik Bawa Singh and Sepoy Piara Singh of 6/14th Punjab Regiment at Wewak on 15th May 1944.

3. Killing Havildar Waryam Singh and Lance-Naik Hazara Singh of 2/12th Frontier Force Regiment at Parom on 27th August 1944.

4. Shooting Sepoy Rulia Singh 2/12th Frontier Force Regiment, Sepoy Kirpa Ram of 6/14th Punjab Regiment near Ain I on 21st, 22nd and 24th October 1944.

5. Shooting eleven Indians, including Havildar Girdhari Lal of 2/12th Frontier Force Regiment, when unable to march at Singu on 1st December 1944.

6. Beheading Jemadar Lachhman Singh of 6/14th Punjab Regiment and Lance Naik Angrezu Ram of 2/12th Frontier Force Regiment at Yawa on 9th January 1945.

7. Shooting Subedars Ishar Singh and Ganda Singh and Jemadars Bahadur Singh and Ram Singh of 2/12th Frontier Force Regiment at Yawa on 1st February 1945.

8. Responsible for all atrocities and deaths of about 200 Indians on the way to the Sepik.

When Lieutenant Mitsuba saw me sitting in the room, his face turned very pale and when these charges were read to him, I could almost read his mind, which showed two trains of thought:

1. He was a bloody fool that he had not killed me.

2. He should not have committed these crimes.

After a little hesitation, when I further submitted more detailed facts, he admitted to all, with the exception of a few, the blame for which he put on to others. He stated the Indians were not tried but were executed summarily by virtue of his powers as a platoon commander. Two of the Indians were killed, he said, because they were the leaders of two groups who were continually fighting amongst themselves and were holding up the work. One of the officers was beheaded for having stolen six bottles of quinine, rations and ammunition and for planning an escape with his men. Others were killed for stealing rations, trying to escape and disobeying orders. He also mentioned some names of other Japanese who had helped him with the executions. There were military photographers and war correspondents at the spot. After finishing the interrogation, Lieutenant Mitsuba was told to salute me and I was told to salute him, as now it was his turn to give the salute. I had saluted him and the Japanese hundreds of times during the two-and-a-half years. I was very happy to think that my long-cherished desire to bring the Japanese to justice was finally meeting with so much success, and the brutal Japanese had to pay for it, but was very sorry at the recollection of the death of my comrades. I think their souls have helped me to take the right retribution and they were also anxiously waiting for this day - "May peace be on them".

On 22nd October 1945, we were given five pounds each to buy necessities. We also went to the barber shop and had our hair cut and dressed in the proper manner – the first time since March 1942. I was told by the natives at Karkar that Major Kudo had killed five Indians at Sangriman in July 1945. On this information, he was brought before the War Crimes Commission and he admitted, with the permission of Lieutenant-General Shoge, he had killed the five Indians. He had found them signalling an Allied aircraft and he had warned them not to do so. They signalled again, as a result of which the aircraft bombed Shoge's headquarters. Shoge then ordered Captains Kobayashi Namio and Nishio Toshihiro to shoot the men.

After this, Lieutenant-General Shoge and these two captains were interrogated. They put the blame on one another and Lieutenant-General Shoge said Major Kudo had reported to him after the execution.

Lieutenant Saito was interrogated with regards to the death of Subedar Rasil Singh and Sepoy Ganga Ram of 3/17th Dogra Regiment and he admitted killing these two men.

On 1st October 1945, Japanese Privates Yasusaka, Tokura and Hibano were interrogated and after a little hesitation they admitted to all their crimes. On this day, I received a letter for the first time since 7th February 1942 (the last letter I received had been from my wife). It was from my friend Lieutenant Hordern who brought us in his barges from Marienberg. This was the loveliest letter and I wish to quote a part of it as follows: -

Lt. Hordern R.A.N.V.R.
H.M.A. M.L. 1347
C/- G.P.O. Australia
28/10/45

My dear Singh,

When I was with you and your men on the river bank at Marienberg, I could see the marks of past sufferings on your faces and bodies and I was amazed at your cheerful disposition and bearing.

It was then that I decided to ask you to share our mess with us until we took you to comfort and security for which you had waited and hoped for so long. You may not know it, but you taught me a great lesson of fortitude and cheerfulness in adversity and it is I who cannot repay this debt to you, so let us say we are both equal on that account.

very sincerely,

Tony Hordern was always very kind to me and tried to keep me happy and forget my past miseries. I am greatly indebted to him.

On this day Lieutenant Murai was brought before the Commission. Smiling gravely through his gold teeth, Murai told the Commission Mamura sat on the chest of Captain Nirpal Chand. Lieutenant Mitsuba pinned his hands to the ground and a third Jap began to strangle him. When his struggles had ceased and he was unconscious, Murai cut off his head. In executing the Indians, he had instructions from Lieutenant Izumi, who had said for any offence against orders or discipline, war prisoners were to be killed without trial. Murai also made these admissions:

1. He had reduced the rations of the Indians who had become too ill and were unable to work. He did this to "make them recover more quickly".

2. When the sick Indians asked for medicine, he told them to eat red ants. He said the natives had told him red ants were a cure for coughing. So when he recommended them to the Indians, he was not being facetious, but merely trying to help them.

3. He admitted that Sepoy Ram Singh of 6/14th Punjab Regiment was tied to a tree and beaten, stabbed and buried. His crime was stealing four lemons from the mission garden. He also admitted previously he had caught Ram Singh stealing vegetables from the garden.

In the evening, Lieutenant Rafferty of 2 N.G.I.B. invited me to his mess. I had a very nice tea. There were many officers there and they were very interested in asking me of my experiences and knowing more about a prisoner's life. They gave me a very enjoyable evening.

On 19th October 1945, other Indians gave their statements regarding the incidents that happened and others which were witnessed by them. I translated them to the Commission and in the evening Captain Smith of 2/3rd Infantry Battalion took me to his mess where I had a very nice tea and a pleasant evening.

Again, the next day, we continued the work and in the evening all the Indians were invited by Lieutenant Murrie to his unit where we received wonderful treatment.

On 11th November there was an identification parade of 165 Japanese. Military history personnel photographed them. All these Japanese had been selected by us as war criminals. There was a touch of fear on every unsmiling face as the camera clicked. All the Japanese were lined up and we pointed out all those who were responsible for torture, murder and cannibalism. Some of my men became very rash when they saw some of the Japanese who had tortured, beaten and been very cruel to 2500 Indians. They were checked from time to time not to push the Japanese but to point at them with their finger. Major-General Iwakiri, Major-General Shoge and Major Kudo were very surprised when I pointed at them. They told the Commission they had not thought of the Indians who were alive. The tables had turned – we were outside of the barbed wire enclosure and they were inside.

In the evening, I was invited by Brigadier Murray Moten, Commander of the 17th Australian Infantry Battalion, to have tea with him. We had a very nice time and he spoke about some of the patrols sent by them to find the Indians. They had given him information about us. I was also informed about this by one of the natives. A few days prior to January 1945, seven Indians were caught by the natives and killed. Therefore, I had lost confidence in them. Brigadier Moten spoke to me a lot about the Indian Army and of the deeds done by it in the world war. He was very proud of it. He expressed his sorrow on account of the Australians not being able to recover more Indians. His brigade had rescued 125 Indians, so I thanked him for that and for feeding and looking after them. He was very pleased to entertain me, as I belonged to the Indian Army, which he described as the greatest army in the world. The words he said at the time of our farewell will always remain in my memory. "You can call me here at any time you like and make yourself as comfortable as though it were home". These words thrilled me with joy and also touched my heart. They meant a lot to me – a miracle of the ears and mind which had not heard like expression for many years past.

It was the happiest day on 12th November 1945, when ten of us Indians were told we would be flying to Rabaul from where we would catch a ship home. They were feeling very happy but sorry to leave me, as I had been detained as a witness of the War Crimes Commission. They told me that I was a lucky man – they had been with me all the time and wanted to go with me again.

In the evening, Sergeant Ron Bader arranged a party for the departing men as he was very fond of them and they were equally fond of him. Other friends from the hospital also joined them and it was a big party. Havildar Hamir Singh expressed his feelings in the following words to the members of the hospital and the division:

"Gentlemen, we think this part of our life which we have passed in your company is the most glorious in our life. The affection and love shown by you is unforgettable in our life. We had forgotten the pleasures of life and how to enjoy them, but you have taught us again and showed us the new light. You always tried to keep us happy, though the problem of understanding each other was a little difficult, yet you never became tired or disgusted with our talk.

We were in hell and according to the views of our religious teachers, the most inhumane people are sent there, where they are beaten by big giants and cannot get to a safe place. They had to walk in swamps and marshes and on sharp thorns on their way. Similar was our fate. We had passed this life of hell, but before we had not seen anybody coming out of it. Now we find this place (hospital) a heaven, and we are firm there is nothing after death, neither hell nor heaven. Everything is here, but it is known only to those who have passed through it.

We are feeling very depressed for missing your lovely society and feeling lonely. You have guided us in a noble way. We had not eaten anything for such a long time and you realised our need for food and offered us special dishes. We also did not shrink from asking you for anything and found ourselves as happy and easy as in our homes. We cannot express our feelings or thoughts for you in such a short time or in your language. The officers and men of your division have done more than they could for our men who have been suffering from the brutalities of the Japanese. Our life is owed to you and your men. We had no contact with Australians before this time and had not the slightest idea of who you are."

Destiny played its role again!

15th November 1945 was a sad day for me and my men – the day of departure. The hospital staff were also very sad, especially Major Widmer and Sergeant Ron Bader. Both of them took a keen interest in our welfare. My ten comrades were ready to fly to Rabaul (New Britain) in order to catch a ship home to India – home which we longed to see. Many of the hospital staff and I accompanied my ten friends to the aerodrome. I was to remain behind as 6th Australian Division needed me as chief witness against the Japanese war criminals.

I had spent most of my perilous days with these ten Indians and missed them as much as they missed me. Their last words as they boarded the plane still echo in my ears "you have guided us magnificently, for three and half years, but now you leave us alone. We are sure that it was your luck which saved us and we miss you very much. Now comes the parting. If we die on the way home, we do not worry as through you we have seen hell and heaven". At the aerodrome they were photographed by many Australians and then the plane took off. We waved to the windows of the plane, from where ten white hand-kerchiefs showed their position and kept waving until the plane went out of sight. Tears came to my eyes and ran swiftly down my cheeks. When I looked at Sergeant Ron Bader, he was in the same position, so we consoled each other and then returned to camp.

The same evening, I said goodbye to the 2/15th Australian Field Ambulance and moved to 6th Australian Division Headquarters, where I shared a tent with Captain Bruce and Lieutenant Rennie. By this time, I was the only Indian left in the Wewak area. The departure of my friends and homesickness worried me at times, but my two tent friends tried their best to keep me happy and assisted me a lot in my undertakings. They succeeded in making me forget the miseries I had suffered and to overlook the loneliness. I used to go to the 104 C.C.S. and visit Sister Kay Murch and Sister Weir and the other members of the staff, who were all very kind to me. Sister Weir gave me a very nice fountain pen, which I still keep with great reverence. They told me to be candid and not to be shy about asking for anything which I needed.

It was not very late in the evening on 16th November 1945 when Captain Bruce and I returned from the pictures and went over to the mess and found Sergeant Ron Bader waiting at the door. I was very surprised to see him there, as he was exhausted and confused. He had walked 5 miles to see me. I asked what was worrying him. He led me to a tent and we sat down. He was very sad and in a low voice told me he had heard news the plane in which my friends were travelling had crashed and all passengers had been killed. It was a great shock to me and made me weep. It still sounded unbelievable to me, so I went to the signals office and asked for confirmation. They signalled to Army HQ in Lae and confirmed the crash. He even told me all the names believed killed. The next morning, I read the following in the paper *"Guinea Gold"* under a big heading:

"28 Believed Killed in New Britain Crash"

"Twenty-eight persons are believed to have lost their lives when an

R.A.A.F. Douglas transport crashed while flying from Jacquinot Bay to Rabaul on Thursday morning 15th November 1945. One of those believed to have been killed was a stowaway. Others were a R.A.A.F. nurse, seven Australian soldiers, three R.A.N. men, six members of the R.A.A.F. including the crew of four and ten Indian POWs who had to catch a ship which would take them home." [22]

This was the tragic end of my dearest friends with whom I had sincere brotherly love. They have left a black spot on my mind forever. When I think of them, I forget all the worldly things which I am enjoying now. They would have been here with me now.

On Sunday I attended a church service at a sac-sac hut at Wewak. Prayers were said for my comrades and a one-minute silence was observed.

A few days after the crash, I received a letter from Lieutenant Monk, who was our first well-wisher and sympathiser after our three and half years of suffering. The letter read as follows:

"Dear Chint Singh,

And now I'll write to you about how I felt on receiving the bad news about the death of your men. Firstly, I must give you (as their officer) my deepest sympathy. Also, I wish to pass on the deep sympathy of my wife and family who also know of the tragedy. They feel they know you quite well my Jemadar, because I sent to them your first letter which you wrote to me. I told them it was one of my valued possessions and they were to look after it until my return.

However, in thinking back, one's thoughts must say at least they did not die in misery and disease. They had suffered terribly, but they had known a great joy and thankfulness when they were rescued and looked

---

22   The R.A.A.F. Douglas C-47 Dakota, Registration A6554 crashed into a 7000-foot mountain, 150 feet below the ridge line shortly after take-off at 0914 hrs on 15th Nov 1945, killing all 28 on board. http://www.planecrashinfo.com/1945/1945-65.htm accessed on 11th Mar 2018.

after by those whom the Great One had singled out for the job. Truly they had known the bitterest despair and misery, but they had also known how good life could be. You must know that too, Jemadar, as you shared their joys and good times at Wewak and it was better for them to die clean, happy and full of hope in an air crash than in the filth and misery of Japanese conditions.

I too have been sending information to Wewak about Japs and I believe one at least will suffer for it. I was very glad to hear of your efforts and know how you will feel that at least you will have paid for some of the lives of the Indians who have been lost.

I will never forget the picture of you and your men as you all came ashore at Angoram. It will be with me as long as I live.

Yours faithfully,

Gerry Monk"

Japanese of Chint Singh guard working on an old road
constructed by him and his party

Japanese of Chint Singh guard working on an old road
constructed by him and his party

Chint Singh writing out his evidence at Headquarters 6 Division for the Wewak
War Crimes Commission, CAPE WOM, NEW GUINEA, 19th Oct 1945
(AWM098105)

Chint Singh points out a Japanese soldier who had mistreated him while he was
PoW to Australian war crimes investigators, 11Sept 1945. (AWM098708)

Chint Singh writing out his evidence at Headquarters 6 Division for the Wewak
War Crimes Commission, CAPE WOM, NEW GUINEA, 19th Oct 1945
(AWM098105)

Lt. General Adachi, GOC Japanese 18th Army outside
the court after given life imprisonment, May 1947

Australian Military Court hearing from the Japanese defence counsel,
trial of Major General Harota, in Rabaul, May 1947

A cemetery of Australian and Indian soldiers at Wewak, New Guinea. The
Australian graveyard commission dugout old graves of Indian POWs with Chint
Singh help and buried them properly in the cemetery December 1945

1945 Christmas at 6 Australian Division Mess, PNG

Chint Singh and his men, happy to survive

Chint Singh and his men being treated at Hospital, 2/15th Field Ambulance,
Boram Beach, Papua New Guinea (AWM098096)

Chint Singh's mates, before boarding the Royal Australian Airforce plane,
which crashed killing all Nov, 1945

Chint Singh and his men being treated at Hospital, 2/15th Field Ambulance, Boram Beach, Papua New Guinea (AWM098096)

Chint Singh and Sister K.J.Murch, i04 C.C.S, Wewak, PNG, December 1945

Chint Singh with his mates and the Australian Nursing staff. (AWM098098)

CHAPTER 9
AUSTRALIAN WAR CRIMES COMMISSION

IT WAS ON 23rd November 1945 that I had my first flight in a Tiger Moth and it was over the Wewak area. Captain Ninkirrow of 6th Division Headquarters took me to the aerodrome and told me all about the aeroplane machines. I learnt where the bombs are kept and how they are released and how the guns are fired. I then had my flight, which lasted for about ten minutes and was at a height of about 5000 feet. It was a lovely flight and I enjoyed it immensely.

On the way back to my quarters, I visited the hospital and came across some Chinese who had also been POWs and had been released by the Australians. They told me they had known some Japanese who had killed and eaten some Indian soldiers in the Maprik area. They said the Japanese belonging to the 41 Engineering Regiment, commanded by Lieutenant Colonel Kato, were those concerned and gave me the names of certain Japanese who were guilty and responsible for the atrocity. I told this to the War Crimes board and they told me to get more information from the Japanese colonel, who was their staff officer. I did this, and consequently the concerned Japanese were brought before the War Crimes Commission, where they admitted to having killed two Indians but said that they had not eaten them.

On 25th November Captain Iraqi who was in charge of the 18th Working Party was interrogated based on the evidence given by me regarding the massacre at But, where 200 Indians were killed or shot in May 1944. He admitted about 205 Indians were left at But when he had marched with the rest of the Indians into the mountains. They were left in charge of Major-General Matsui. He had heard that about the end of May 1944, the Indians had signalled an Allied aircraft and directed them to bomb the Japanese main positions. One American submarine had appeared on the surface near the Indian camp and some of the Indians attempted to swim to it, but the Japanese outpost opened fire and the ship submerged. The Indian camp was encircled by the Japanese Military Police, who opened fire on the Indians. Most of the Indians died there, a few escaped.

The following day Captain Izumi of the 19th Working Party was interrogated in connection with his instructions to wild natives to ridicule the Indians. He said he knew a native named Mumbigo whom he had made headman of the natives. On one occasion, he beat two Indians to such an extent they died a few days later.

On 29th November 1945, I missed one of my friends, namely Lieutenant Murray, very much. Captain Bruce and I had dinner with him in the 2/3rd Battalion's mess. There was a nice party in the evening and Captain Smith and other officers of the battalion entertained me very well. The place I had hated and where I had suffered only a few months before became an interesting and lovely place. The sages have said "He can change a desert into a valley and a valley into a desert".

It was the 30th November 1945 that the first Australian Military Court gathered in Wewak for the trial of Lieutenant Tazaki, who had been charged with cannibalism for the killing and eating of an Australian soldier. There were many photographers in the court, plus two correspondents and a large audience. The court consisted of the following:-

President –
Lieutenant-Colonel Cameron—*2/2nd Battalion*

Members –
Lieutenant-Colonel Hutchinson—*2/3rd Battalion*

Lieutenant-Colonel Neville—*4th Battalion*

Major Fogarty—*Headquarters 6 Australian Division*

Judge-Advocate Major Corr—*Headquarters 6 Australian Division*

Prosecutor Captain Roy Steele

Defending Captain Watson.

At the beginning of the court, an oath on the Bible was taken and the Crown Prosecutor and the witness took the oath. Lieutenant Tazaki came in with two other Japanese officers who had been sent by General Adachi to assist him. The witnesses were called in one by one and the proceedings were translated to the accused. The court then adjourned for lunch and resumed later. The accused was asked to state his version of the affair. He told the court he was very hungry and weak. Moreover, he was very wild, as fourteen of his men had been killed in the action of that day. The defending officer defended him on the grounds the accused was under the pressure of constant artillery fire, hunger and weakness and his mind was unsettled, hence he ate the flesh. The court adjourned until the following day.

At the start of the court the next day, the accused was found guilty on both charges. The long process of discussion and pleading was annoying me very much as many times I had seen my comrades bayoneted and finally beheaded for minor mistakes, such as stealing four lemons, a bottle of quinine, a few cakes of soap and even a handful of rice. But never were they given the chances to plead. The Japanese privates were allowed to kill an Indian POW at any time and in any way they liked. There are many concrete examples of this, even admitted by the Japanese themselves. They had very mercilessly murdered the Indian prisoners of war in New Guinea. Now the same Japanese were being met with such a justice as they had no right to receive. The defending officer pleaded that severe punishment should not be imposed on Tazaki. The judge advocate put on the matter before the court and it closed for the finding of the verdict. When the court again resumed, the sentence was promulgated, and the audience was pleased when the death penalty was passed. Death by hanging.

On 2nd December, I met one of the officers of the War Crimes Commission and pointed out some of the graves of my men and also showed him the place where about 200 Indians were cremated. I also gave him the names and units of those cremated and requested he put a signboard or some other marker to indicate the place.

Sergeant Niama of the 16th Working Party was interrogated a few days later. He admitted about 220 Indian POWs were shot in May 1944 at But for signalling Allied aircraft. He explained a Japanese major of the local guard had done that. The major was called in the next day and he admitted having done the above, as signalling the aircraft made it bad for the Japanese and it did a lot of damage.

That afternoon, I went for tea with Captain Roy Steele to the 16th Brigade Headquarters mess. The officiating brigadier, Lieutenant-Colonel Cameron, greeted me very kindly. He told me how he had escaped from New Britain with his men in 1942 and how later about 40 of his men were captured by the Japanese at Madang (New Guinea) and tied to the trees and bayoneted. He also told me other stories of rape and inhuman actions against the civil and military personnel. We had a very nice evening and laughed at the jokes of Captain Roy Steele, who was humorous all the time. He is a nice jolly man and had helped me a lot and had been very interested in my affairs. He was a solicitor and came from Melbourne.

From the 5th to 15th December 1945, most of my time was taken up by interrogations at the Military Court. I also made contact with Lieutenant Monk (in charge of the interior posts) to send patrols to search the jungle and swamps for any other Indians, which he did, but without result. He sent some natives who had seen Indians being killed by the Japanese. The Japanese were lined up and five criminals were picked out. I made enquiries from some of the natives in the surrounding area and it was confirmed 128 sick Indians of my party, who had been left at Parom, were murdered by the Japanese.

On 12th December, many of my Australian friends went back to Australia and the Wewak area lost its life. My tent-mate, Captain Bruce, left by his boat and I felt very dejected and home-sick. But my duty was not yet over. There were still many Japanese left who had to be interrogated. Lieutenant Marsden Hordern of M.L. 1347 also left for Brisbane. I missed him very much as I had enjoyed good times with him and made so many friends on the deck of his tiny yellow boat. My first voyage on this boat after my recovery will forever remain in my memory. Captain Smith of 2/3rd Battalion and some of my other friends also left for home. Now it was very hard to pass the time, but Captain Roy Steele, Lieutenant Clarrie Stone and Sergeant Ron Bader and the sisters in the hospital were still looking after me very well. Sergeant Ron Bader presented me with a chess set, a gift that I appreciate very much.

On 22nd December Lieutenant-General Adachi, supreme commander of the Japanese 18th Imperial Army in New Guinea, and his staff officers were interrogated in connection with the instructions issued to his units in charge of Indian POWs. Previously, many Japanese officers had stated they had received instructions from General Adachi, giving them authority to execute Indians without trial. Lieutenant-General Adachi said as Japanese Imperial Headquarters could not send legal officers for court martials because of the blockade of New Guinea, he had issued personal orders that the Japanese Military code be administered by local commanders in New Guinea. Acts for which death penalty could be imposed were specified as rebellion in the face of the enemy, desertion, cannibalism and signalling aircraft.

He was shown a list of offences which included stealing food and medicine and he said he personally thought the only offences worthy of death penalty were signalling allied aircraft, cannibalism and refusing orders.

At his interrogation, Major-General Shoge admitted it was reported to him by Major Kudo that he had beheaded five Indians for signalling the enemy aircraft. He also stated had Major Kudo reported this to him earlier, he would not have executed them. Major-General Shoge stated Major Kudo was not justified in executing the Indians prior to getting his sanction and he was very annoyed with Major Kudo over this hasty step.

I finished most of my work before Christmas and had a wonderful holiday attending parties every evening. This was the first Christmas for the world to enjoy after six years of suffering. We had no food for Christmas 1944, but were living on grass and other wild things. Our number then was reduced from 539 to 43 and it appeared not one of us had any chance of remaining alive until Christmas 1945. But there was a light of hope for finishing our journey. I remember well the words to my men "Somebody out of us will see and enjoy the next Christmas". Little did I realise t I was to be the only Indian of that group to enjoy the Christmas of 1945. I was very upset and despondent over my ten comrades, who I had lost in the plane crash.

Christmas Eve was celebrated in the most splendid way in the Sergeants' Mess of the 2/15th Australian Field Ambulance. The commanding officer, Major Widmer, and Sergeant Ron Bader greeted me and entertained me. It was a lovely evening on the beach at Wewak where we had worked for two-and-a-half years as labourers. It was a strange world to live in and think of. I was invited by all the units in the 6th Division. My days were spent with Captain Steele and Lieutenant Stone, always visiting the units in a jeep. The native boys of 2nd New Guinea Infantry Battalion performed a very nice sing-

sing (dance and song). They were dressed in wildflowers and leaves from trees. The commanding officer of the unit presented me with a Christmas card and some photos of his unit in action. The card read as follows: -

"Christmas Greetings"

The Commanding Officer, Officers and Non-Commissioned Officers of 2 New Guinea Infantry Battalion extend hearty good wishes for Christmas 1945 and express sincere hope that the New Year will see the ties of war cemented by peace.

2 New Guinea Infantry Battalion

25/12/45

To Jemadar Chint Singh of the Indian Army, with all the best wishes for many years to come and hoping that the friendship of your country and ours will continue for all time.

Signed John H. Pawson. Major. Officiating Commander 2.N.G.I.B.

I was heartily welcomed to all units in the 6th Australian Division. Captain Steele, Lieutenant Stone and I were invited by the nursing sisters to their mess and they gave a very nice party. Sister Kay Murch presented me with a turban which she had made from some material. I was asked to tie it in their presence and they were very interested to see me perform the task. When I put on the turban, I became a figurehead in the division and consequently had to demonstrate many times a day. I receive many Christmas cards and greetings from many friends.

I also wished happy Christmas to the place where I lived for two years under the terrible conditions as a Japanese prisoner of war. I felt as though the place itself was wishing me a happy Christmas as the spirits of my comrades had moved free from Japanese aggression. I found the little hole where I would hide myself from the American bombings. Old, sad memories were renewed, and the tears rolled down my cheeks. I was the only Indian left in the area now, whereas there were about 2,000 during the past two Christmases. About 2,800 Indians had lost their lives in this area.

On 31st December Captain Steel, Major Corr and I were invited to the A.O.D. Mess for dinner as the commanding officer had arranged a big party (He asked me to do the "Indian rope trick"). In the afternoon we prepared for it and had a rehearsal. In the evening, the guests started arriving and celebrations commenced. There was a lot of singing and amusement until midnight when all joined and we sang the New Year's song (Auld Lang Syne). Then the commanding officer addressed the gathering, saying he had brought with great difficulty one Indian magician for the occasion. He told them I was the only Indian magician in the South-West Pacific who could perform the Indian rope trick. He called for me and I went near the place where the rope was kept. I then recited a few verses in the Hindi language and acted the part of a magician. According to the pre-arranged scheme, I signalled to the man outside to pull the string and the rope stood up like the snake's hood. Then started cheers, laughing and chatting. In this way, I took part in the celebrations for welcoming the New Year of 1946 and I thoroughly enjoyed it.

On New Year's Day, I was invited by the hospital staff. We had been looked after by them better than their own patients, resulting in our rapid recovery. After two months of careful treatment, it was hard to say we had been POWs and had suffered much. I was very touched by the kind works of Sister Kay Murch when one day I thanked her for her kindness. She said, "Chint Singh, you and your people have suffered so much for me for so many years, so now it is my turn to help you and make you forget all the sufferings you have undergone". One can imagine if such are the feelings of any individual in a nation or country, how proud and lucky are those who have fought for them. I have come in contact with many men and women of Australia and I am very much pleased to find the same feeling in most of them.

On the morning of 4th January 1946 Lieutenant Fong and 21 other Chinese ex-prisoners of war, who had been brought from Hong Kong by the Japanese and used as forced labour at Wewak, left for Rabaul to catch a ship home. They were very nice and humorous boys. They were given charge of about fifty Japanese who were employed for camp duties by the 6th Division Headquarters. These Chinese boys used to make a lot of fun of the Japanese. Lieutenant Fong is a very nice person and comes from a respectable family in Hong Kong. The rest of my day was spent with some friends on a beautiful picnic. Coincidently, a native appeared with a big fish in one hand and a spear in the other and as I got closer, I recognised him to be one of those who had helped me at Rainimbo, when I was a prisoner of war. His name was Tambkabun and he had given me many things secretly. We were overjoyed to see each other again. He offered me the fish and said to my Australian friends, "Me save this pella India cap am I Japan calibu stop. Me give im something belong to kai-kai, me sorry tumas, plenty India ungry idie pinis. Japan man give him nothing belonga kai-kai." (I know this Indian Officer. He was a prisoner in Japanese hands. I used to give him some food, but many Indians died of starvation. The Japanese had given them nothing to eat).

My friends were very impressed with his politeness and manners. They said, "These natives are far better than the civilised Japanese". I gave him a few cigarettes, a match box, a little bread and a fish tin and he was very pleased indeed and went on his way with his spear at the alert, watching for more prey.

I then gathered together a few twigs and built a fire and demonstrated how I used to cook fish in the fire whilst I was a POW. My friends were very interested and helped me pack the fish in leaves. When the fish was cooked, I unpacked it and shared it around and then listened to the compliments, which were passed by all as they greatly appreciated it. Lieutenant Stone demanded more of my share. It was a very enjoyable day and we returned home in the evening.

My time continued to be very pleasant until 13th January 1946.

On the evening of 12th January, there was a very nice party in the 6th Division Headquarters mess, in my honour. Major Corr, Captain Steele and Lieutenant Stone had made the arrangements and we had a great night with plenty of singing and fun.

CHAPTER 10
JOURNEY BACK HOME

ON 13TH JANUARY 1946, I said goodbye to my tent and my many friends in Division Headquarters. Lieutenant Stone drove me to 104 C.C.S. where Sister Kay Murch and Miss Jean Robertson had prepared tea for us (Miss Robertson is now Mrs. C. Stone). I had a very nice tea and then they accompanied me to the airstrip. Sergeant Ron Bader and other friends were there, and we had a long chat before I noticed my luggage being loaded on to the plane. I could read from my friends' faces they were going to miss me very much. The happiness which I had to go home changed to sadness and it became very hard for me to depart. They had proved to be real friends and true comrades in my adversity and had helped and shared in all of my adventures in the last four months. Tears came to my eyes when I wished them goodbye and got aboard the plane. When the plane took off, I could see tiny fingers waving white handkerchiefs, but within a few seconds we were up in the air and I had lost them from my vision. Then I took a last look at Wewak, at the sunken Japanese ships and barges in the sea and all the places so familiar to me. Once again, the sad memories of life as a prisoner of war came into my mind. What a change of life it was for me, but not for the other 2,800 Indians I had left calm and quiet forever in the swamps of New Guinea. I realised how lucky I was to experience those changes.

The plane in which I was travelling was a R.A.A.F. Douglas transport. It was travelling at a height of 8000 feet, 90 miles per hour and with 26 passengers aboard. I was enjoying the scenery with the greatest of enthusiasm. The plane called at Madang, Finschafen and finally at Lae. This was the first long journey I had ever had in my life and it was quite comfortable and very enjoyable.

When we arrived at Lae, I reported my arrival to the Army movement control where I was told I would have to wait two days for a plane to take me to Australia, therefore I had to find accommodation and settle there. I went to Lae proper and visited its surroundings but did not find much difference when comparing it with Wewak except it was more stabilised. Captain Zwar (who was a doctor at Wewak) visited me and we had a long chat. I also met another doctor there, namely Captain Kenneth Sowden, who was going to Brisbane, Australia and in the time I knew him, we became closely associated. On the morning of 16th January, Captain Sowden and I were taken to the airstrip and the plane took off at 0600 hours. The weather was extremely bad and the engines of the plane were roaring and very audible. There were very thick layers of clouds over the mountains and the jungles. Consequently, I felt very cold and felt like putting on warmer clothes. After having been in the air for six and a half hours, we were given our first glimpse of the North-East Coast of Australia, the land which my comrades and I had longed to see. But alas, I and only a few others were destined to see its beauties.

Cairns, a small town on the north-east coast, was the first spot I put my feet on Australian soil. This town was the first I had seen since we left Singapore. We obtained transport and were driven to a very nice hotel in the town where we had an enjoyable lunch. I was so surprised to see so many factories in such a small town.

We left Cairns and went to Townsville where we had to change as the plane did not go any further than there. The trip to Townsville was very enjoyable and I enjoyed the scenery of green fields, pastures and small villages very much. When we arrived at Townsville, Captain Sowden saw a Dutch plane ready to take off for Brisbane, so he arranged with the pilot to take us. This plane was more comfortable than the R.A.A.F. transports. On this plane we were served tea and biscuits by a Dutch air hostess. This plane flew at a greater speed and at 2030 hours I saw my first glimpses of Brisbane. It was very lovely to see from the sky, especially the straight lines of lights crossing each other on the roads and lanes. I would have liked to have seen it for a longer time, but the plane landed on the aerodrome.

Captain Sowden advised me to go and stay in the officers' club and promised to come and see me on the following morning. I accepted his advice and went to the club in the air transport vehicle and obtained a comfortable room. In the club I met an Australian gentleman who had been a prisoner of war in Singapore and had recently been released. He was a lieutenant in the Australian army. His name was R. Livingstone. He took me for a walk in the city and showed me many places of importance and introduced me to many friends. I was welcomed everywhere I went. It was after midnight I returned to the club and I felt happy I had been able to enjoy so many things which were so new to me. I had come from the jungles after having spent almost 3 years in the subordination of the wild Japanese and had not been used to the sympathetic and kind words of human beings for all that time. It was all so wonderful to me. It was there and then I craved to meet an Indian with whom I could converse in my mother language, which I had not spoken for the last three months. I wished to express in Hindustani to someone all I had learnt and seen in one of the capital cities of Australia. This craving was so strong I was able to overcome it by sitting down at a table and writing a letter to my wife and family and telling them all about it and my experiences in Brisbane that evening.

Next morning, Lieutenant Livingstone took me in his car for a ride into the country and then to his home, which was in one of the suburbs. He had a nice little home, clean and well decorated. He was not married then, but had all the arrangements made for a future date. He served me with fruit and cool drinks. The country is undulating and gave a very nice view from his place. When we returned to the club, I found Lieutenant Rafferty (an old friend from Wewak days) waiting for me, and we were very pleased to see each other and enjoyed a ride around the city together. In the morning, I went to the movement control officer and was told I had to fly to Sydney.

When I arrived back at the club, I received a telephone call from Capt. Sowden telling me to wait for him, which I did and in no time he and his wife came to receive me. Mrs Sowden greeted me very kindly, as she was happy to see me alive and with such an experience. They took me for tea to their house and there I met their parents, who were old and gentle people. It was the first time after five years I had dined with a family and the first time in my life I had dined with an Australian family. I was served with various delicious meals and enjoyed them very much. I chatted with them for about three hours and obtained much pleasure from it.

On 18th January 1946, I left Hotel Daniell officer's club, Brisbane, boarded a plane for Sydney and on the way had a good aerial view of the eastern side of Australia, seeing many farms and large cattle herds. We reached Sydney at 1130 hours and again I reported my arrival to the movement control officer, who in turn told me I would have to wait for further instructions from General Headquarters, Melbourne. Captain Barlow (Q and movement control staff captain) took me in his staff car to the Showgrounds Military Camp, and I was given a room in the Cooper's Dip. The very name of this place is tickling to the reader and whenever I think of it, I laugh. Cooper's Dip is a small building with five or six rooms and was used by Australian officers on the move who had a day or two to spend there. My friends, who I met later, also laughed at the name of the place.

I made a telephone call to Captain Bruce and Lieutenant Murrie and they were very surprised to hear I was in Sydney. I had my meals in the officers' mess and the officers were very kind to me. Major Smith and Captain Barlow helped me a great deal.

The following morning, I met with Lieutenant-Colonel Mint, the chief legal officer of New South Wales, and although he was very busy, he afforded me some spare time to talk with me about the various aspects of life. He arranged for transport to take me to the city and all other important places of interest. When I came back to Cooper's Dip, I found Captain Bruce and his daughter Jeanette waiting for me in their car. Captain Bruce told me to take everything with me to their house and I was to stay with them as long as I wished. Captain Bruce had met another friend of mine, Lieutenant Marsden Hordern, who had invited us all for tea, so I hurriedly packed my bags and in no time we had gone through the city and were at Lieutenant Hordern's house. The father, mother and other members of the family greeted me and it was a very nice meeting as it was a long time since I had left Hordern at Wewak. Soon after Lieutenant Wilkinson also joined us (The readers might remember that these two officers were on the boat M.L. 1347, which had been brought up to Wewak after our release on the Sepik River. They had proved to be very kind to me and my comrades). I was given a nice party which I enjoyed very much. We then left and drove to Captain Bruce's home.

There I found Captain Bruce's wife and little girl Heather waiting for me. They then guided me to a nice and well-furnished room which had been allotted for my use. The house itself was very nice and with a small orchard. My host did not spare any pains in entertaining me and I had a very pleasant evening meal. Some of their friends and relatives joined us after tea and once again we had a pleasant time. Next day my hosts took me in their car to show me the important places of the city. Lieutenant Murrie also accompanied us. Again, this country was very undulating, and it was very spectacular when the car was at some height from where could be seen a wonderful picture of the city and the Sydney Harbour Bridge. I was also impressed with Manly Beach, as there were thousands of people swimming and enjoying life. All of these forms of recreations were interesting, as I had never seen them before. There were even seats made so one could sit and enjoy the scenery. Bondi Beach was also visited, but I did not like it as much as I did Manly, although many people in Sydney speak highly of Bondi. Another thing which was nice for me and impressed me was the underground railway system in the city. It is worth adopting in the big cities. The steps, working automatically, were taking the people up and down – it certainly is a nice system. The connection by trams is very convenient, as the passengers have to wait only a short time.

The Sydney Harbour Bridge is also fascinating and unique in its structure. It is very large and spans a stretch of sea. Big ships pass underneath it quite easily. The railways, tramways and vehicular traffic have their own roads and passages across the top.

I met Mrs Steel as previously arranged and she took us to her house, where we had a very nice afternoon tea. From her house, the harbour looked very nice. She pointed out the places where Japanese midget submarines were caught in the net and finally destroyed by the Royal Australian Navy.

Captain Bruce's parents lived about six miles from them, so we paid them a visit. His father was 61 years of age, a very strong and hard worker and interested in plants. In his orchard he had very many different types of plants which had come from other countries.

Sydney is the oldest city in Australia and is famed for its Harbour Bridge. I visited the war memorial, which had been erected in memory of those who had sacrificed their lives in the Great War 1914-1918. I also visited the public gardens, which I must admit were very well worth seeing, as from there a good view of the harbour can be seen. I was also taken to the zoo and saw such animals as the koala bear, zebras and kangaroos, all these being very strange to me. The zoo was very fascinating and was built on a large scale.

The news I was in Sydney reached Captain Smith, who came to

see me after a great struggle. He came to show me around the city and one important place which I saw was the aeroplane factory at Liverpool. There I noticed many aeroplanes lying idle and upon enquiring about them I was informed that now the war was over they were going to be destroyed as they were only a burden to the government and required a lot of money to maintain them. Captain Smith also took me past many farms and I noticed the people were working very hard on them. The farming in Australia is very modern and with small labour they get great production.

Mrs Bruce's parents invited me out to dinner and there I also met her sisters. They had a very nice home built on the banks of Cook's River (This river is named after the great explorer James Cook who sailed around South America and discovered Mercury Bay, Society Islands, Friendly Islands and the south east part of Australia. He sailed up this river and for the first time surveyed the area around it inland). The scenery was so pleasing and the air so fresh while I was there, I could not refrain from having a sleep so I took a nap. We then had a nice dinner and then left.

Then we were invited into the house of Mrs Bruce's sister and again, a very pleasant time we had. There I met an ex-POW from Singapore, so we had a very long chat over events of the past and present.

The next day I met Lieutenants Moore and Rafferty, who took me to the pictures, botanical gardens and a few other places of interest. It was hard to get into the pictures as the theatres were rushed. After the show we went to a hotel where again we found everything busy. However, after waiting for a while, we were able to get a table and sit and eat.

The people of Australia are rich and have a high standard of living. They are very free in all their dealings as the prices are fixed and there is little chance of cheating. There is a control on prices and articles but the black market, which is very prevalent, and which was very new to me, was working all right. It was in Sydney I learned for the first time in my life about the rationing and controlling of things.

The population of Australia is only 8,000,000 and the country is much larger than India and full of resources, therefore, the people are making better use of it. Women and girls work in the hotels, shops, factories, offices and are driving cars and taxis and doing various other jobs. Hence, their labour is cheaper, and they are preferred in many positions. Of course, most of the production is done by machines which increase the output a lot. Most of the commodities required for consumption in Australia are procured from their own resources and in addition, there are large stores ready for export. Seating capacity in hotels and theatres is always very rushed and one must wait their turn, however as far as the pictures are concerned, one can book ahead.

The people of Australia are white and mostly from British decent. In the beginning it was inhabited by natives, however when its resources became known to the British and discoveries had been made, they started immigration, which is still being carried out to this day. The people are very good and hospitable. There is, of course, the bad sect but then in comparison with the population they are not noticeable. That is the case in every country. There were some cases of robbery and murder while I was in Sydney, but they were only few.

Recreations and forms of amusement are plentiful in Australia and the people are very fond of them. Races (horse) are a very popular sport and it is interesting to see the different reactions of the people, some tearing up tickets, others cursing horses, while others are very happy with having had a win, earnings for bar expenses in the evening. Once I was taken to the races and I saw a tall, slim woman who had put some money on a horse. She told me it was a good horse and suggested I too put some money on it, but I refused, saying I was not interested. However, she persisted, so I had a bet, but all was in vain as the horse came home second last. She was very annoyed and tearing up her ticket, hurried away saying "bad luck".

Sunday in Australia is observed as a holiday and the people do very little work, only in their homes and have most of the time for recreation, such as going to the beach, the zoo, for a walk or playing some sport. The streets are full of people and the market for buying is wide.

On 27th January there was a reunion party of the Bruces and his three brothers and a sister who live in the other cities were present for the party. It was very pleasant too. There we had many photos taken by Captain Bruce's father.

I was taken by Mr Ayson (brother-in-law of Mrs Bruce) to the pictures and then to his home, which is situated on a small ridge and affords a great view. Attached to the home was an orchard from which Mr Ayson gets many vegetables. He served as a soldier in the Great War and has a great interest for soldiers. He has two children; the son having served in the army and the daughter who is married. His daughter had just had a baby, so the next week we visited the maternity hospital. I was informed at the time of delivery of the baby all women in Australia go to such hospitals. There are very few deaths at the time of birth in Australia, but the figures in India are horrible.

My time spent in Sydney was very enjoyable, as my friends were forever entertaining me. By this time, I had seen enough of Sydney and I was very anxious to get home and see my people. I requested the air movement control send me home as soon as possible. But it was not easy to get a plane to India as they went only once a week and there were so many people with high priority who had been waiting for several days. I then started to call upon Major Smith (officer of the camp), Captain Barlow and Lieutenant Barrett (air movement) to send me soon and they were good to me and helped me a lot.

At last I received orders on 4th February 1946 to fly to India by the evening service. Hurriedly, I packed my bags and said goodbye to my hosts. The two little girls, Heather and Jeanette, were wishing me goodbye and waving their hands until I lost them from sight as we took the bend of the road. I reported to the air movement control in the Orient Line Building and was pleased to see Sister Kay Murch and Lieutenant and Mrs Clarrie Stone waiting for me. I gathered my necessary documents and then Sister Murch took us out to a delicious dinner. They then stayed with me until 2030 hours, when I got into the air transport vehicle, which took me to the aerodrome. As we drove away, I could see their smiling faces gradually disappear in the distance.

It was 2100 hours on 4th February 1946 that I reached the Sydney aerodrome. A Liberator with 15 other passengers was ready to take me to my loved ones who I had not seen for five years and about who I knew of no changes. I booked in my cargo and was given an air travel ticket.

Within a short time, I was in the plane and the plane was airborne and we then received our instructions of safety precautions from a Flight Lieutenant. It was a beautiful night, very moonlit and scary. I was feeling sad about having to leave my friends in Sydney.

During the night, I had a comfortable trip. The plane was travelling at about 200 m.p.h. and the height was 10,000 feet, however, I cannot form any opinion about the country over which we passed, as it was dark. Tea and toast were served on the plane.

When dawn broke, I learned we were flying over Western Australia. Most of the country then was very barren and full of shrubs, however, I later started to see the pasture lands and rich green fields with many sheep grazing on them. It was 0815 hours that I had my first glimpse of the suburbs and city of Perth. It was very lovely from the air so early in the morning; the river flowing through the city made a very picturesque sight. The plane landed after the 2100-mile journey.

We alighted and were taken to the mess in the air transport vehicle where we had our breakfast. We were allowed to visit the city until the evening. I went into the city and had a long walk and a ride and found it interesting. It is not as big or as full of life as Sydney, but is more modern and better situated. We visited one of the beaches and enjoyed the swimming a lot. I met a few sailors from the British Aircraft Carrier *Implacable* who had spent some time with Indian troops in the Middle East. They spoke very highly of the Indians in the area and told me of their many adventures. In the evening, I returned to the aerodrome.

At 2230 hours the plane again took off and within a short time we were flying out over the ocean. I could see nothing but the water below. The following morning at 0630 hours the plane circled over a small swampy island which I later found out to be Cocos, an island which I had heard so many times in my geography lessons but have never dreamed that I would see. It was a very small and unhealthy island. However, we landed on the drome and were taken to the mess for breakfast. Water was very scarce, so much in fact we could not get any to shave or wash ourselves with. Soon after breakfast, the plane again took off and this time for Colombo. At about 1600 hours, we had a vision of Ceylon and soon the plane had passed over the Western Coast and had landed, after having completed about 3,400 miles from Perth. I then said goodbye to the pilot and the crew and reported to movement control. I was informed I would have to wait a few days for a plane. I searched for an Indian regiment and was told the 26th Dogra Battalion was stationed at Normandy camp. I then rang the adjutant and arranged for accommodation with them for my stay in Ceylon and he was pleased and told me I would be made very welcome. This pleased me, so I hastened my trip to the camp of the 26th Dogras.

I was received by the head clerk and jamadar-adjutant at the gate and was then taken to the subedar-major. After having talked with them for some time, they fixed up my accommodation and I then had a hot bath. Indian food was served to me, for which I was well prepared after four years without it. After this, I was taken to the Indian pictures which I enjoyed. All of the actors were new and I noticed a great difference from the pictures I used to see in 1941. I met some boys from my village, but I would not have recognised them had they not given me some of their particulars. I learned to my greatest joy everyone in my home was all right, so all my worries about my family were forgotten on this day.

My Australian friends would say to me "no news is good news" and it proved to be true. I at once wrote letters to everybody (After my recovery on 30th September 1945 I had written many letters home but had not received a reply. Only my friend Ron Bader had one letter from my brother, but it had not conveyed any news of the family hence I would worry very much). I also wrote letters to my friends in Australia telling them all about my journey and then the news of my family in which they were interested. I was pleased to hear about all the changes in my village and all the strange stories. It pleased me much to know a girls' school had been opened in the village. There were some men in the 26th Dogra that had relatives in New Guinea and I knew to have died there. As they had no definite information about the deceased, I told them all about it. There was a big party next evening and the pipe band played for about four hours. All the officers talked with me about my experiences.

Next day I visited the city but found it very dull and uninteresting when comparing them with the cities of Australia. There were many people walking the streets with bare feet and the streets were very dirty. I stayed in Colombo for three days and in that time saw much of the city.

On 11th February 1946, I said goodbye to my hosts and went to the aerodrome at 0630 hours. The plane left for India and the vision of Southern India was very thrilling to me and I felt as though I could kiss the land. I saluted her as I saluted the day. I had said goodbye on 11th April 1941, leaving Madras (now Chennai) for overseas deployment. I thanked the Almighty Father for my safe return and offered a little prayer sitting in the plane. We landed at Cochin at 0930 hours. I found the country changed a lot. I met many Indians and read many notice boards with great interest, hoping to learn everything in a day. But there had been too many changes to learn in a day or two.

I had my tea and the plane again took off after an hour. We passed over the Deccan mountains and landed at Bangalore for lunch. Soon after lunch we set off and were once again over the Deccan plateau.

At about 1630 hours, the plane landed at Santa Cruz aerodrome, Bombay. I was taken to Juhu air transit camp for the night.

I was surprised to see things in Bombay were dearer than in Australia. In the evening, I visited the city but did not find it as interesting as I did in 1939. Everything was very costly, and I lamented on not having bought my necessities in Australia.

The following morning, the plane took us to Karachi after having followed the coast from Bombay. I had an aerial view of Karachi and its surroundings, but I did not find it very impressive. The lunch in the mess was much below the standard I used to get in Australia.

At Karachi, I changed planes for Delhi. This time we passed over the desert of Rajputana and landed at Jodhpur. In some places I could see wheat crops, but most of the country was barren and shrubby, like Central Australia. Jodhpur is an Indian state and is governed by a *Rajah* (king). His palace is beautiful and is built on the side of a hill near the aerodrome. I saw it from a distance.

I finished my journey at Delhi on 12th February 1946 after having completed almost 8,000 miles. I was accommodated in the air booking centre. The cost of meals was more than in Bombay, but I was happy to reach the capital of my country for which I had dreamed of for so many years.

The next day I went to movement control and was issued with a rail warrant to proceed to my Regimental Centre at Sialkot (now in Pakistan). I then hurried to the station and got the train, which was going to Lahore (now in Pakistan). It was pleasant to go by the train through the lovely plains of the Punjab. I was feeling very cold too as I had not experienced a winter season for the last five years. I arrived at Lahore on 14th February at 1430 hours and changed for Sialkot where I reached at 2200 hours. I was pleased to pass through so many stations so well known to me. I was welcomed in the regiment and had long talks with my old friends. There were many changes in the regiment. The educated soldiers who had been with me in India had got King's Commissions and the others who were not so well educated had been promoted to Subedars and Jemadars. I was pleased to see them but was also very envious.

In the morning, I met the commanding officer, the second-in-command and the adjutant. They were glad to see me and congratulated me on my success. I submitted to them all my news and information about those people who had been killed and told them all the important matters. The commanding officer had many letters from my family asking him of my whereabouts, but nothing was known to anybody until I was recovered by the Australians and was able to send my first cable on 15th October 1945. The commanding officer ordered the adjutant to arrange for my leave. I was given three months leave, so I immediately caught the train back to home.

The last letter I had written was from Colombo and my family had no knowledge of when I would arrive there. I finally reached my hometown on 19th February at 1300 hours. I had a good reception in the town and many people gathered to ask me many questions, many of which were left unanswered as I had to reach my home by night and I was in a hurry. On the outskirts of my village, I met many friends who accompanied me to my house to congratulate my mother and wife, who had a harrowing time for five years.

As soon as I reached my house, my mother, who was sick in her bed, got out and embraced me. Tears of joy rolled down her cheeks. After that day, she recovered her health fully. My wife and other members of the family came in turn and embraced me. The village band was called in and the rejoicings went on in the house. Indian sweets were distributed to the people and after a few days there was a big feast. In a way, I was a newborn baby in the house. Many friends and relatives would come and see me and hear my story.

Chint Singh with Ron Bader,
the first Australian nurse to treat Indian POWs.1945

Chint Singh with Ron Bader, in Perth, 1947

Lt. Monk, the first Australian officer who met Chint Singh after being rescued

Chint Singh with Mr. and Mrs. Monk in Melbourne, April 1947

Chint Singh with Lt. Moore in Botanical Garden, in Sydney February 1946

Chint Singh with Capt. Dough Bruce, of 30th Australian Infantry Bn.
at his house in Sydney, January 1946

Chint Singh with Capt. Bruce's daughters Jeanette and Heather, during his stay with the family for 2 weeks in January, 1946

Chint Singh with Lt. C. Stone of 2/3 Australian Infantry Battalion at Cape Wom, PNG, January 1946.

Chint Singh with Capt. Smith and Lt C. Stone near the Mess of 6 Division
Headquarters, at Cape Wom, PNG, January 1946

Chint Singh with Capt. Smith's family, in Melbourne in 1947

CHAPTER II

RECALLED AS CHIEF DIRECT WITNESS

THE STORY NOW goes to 1947 and centres around Rabaul. I was recalled by the Australian Government to give evidence against the Japanese generals on trial for atrocities, ill-treatment of POWs in the Wewak and New Guinea area. I am glad God has given me this opportunity of avenging the deaths of my comrades in a lawful and right way. I was happy to visit Australia again, just one year after I had left it. It was a great pleasure to me and my friends to meet again so unexpectedly. Again, they gave me a pleasant stay in Sydney.

I am also glad justice had been laid on all the criminals and approximately 50 have been hanged and about 100 are serving terms of imprisonment ranging from 5 years to 20 years. The most interesting case is that of Lieutenant-General Hatazo Adachi, General Officer Commanding 18th Japanese Imperial Army in New Guinea under whose command were about 3,000 Indian POWs, of which only 11 were handed over when Adachi surrendered to the Australians in September 1945. He had denied the fate of others until he and his subordinates were charged by me and the rest of my comrades before the Australian War Crimes Commission.

Lt. General Adachi was charged with failing to control the conduct of his subordinates, who committed brutal atrocities and other crimes against the forces of Australia and its allies. The crimes which were admitted in the area under Adachi's command by his subordinates were murder and ill-treatment of Indian, Australian and American POWs and of native and Chinese civilians. Besides this, there was cannibalism and mutilation of the above-mentioned forces.

The court was comprised of Australian military personnel as follows –

President. Major-General T.S. Whitelaw, Brigadier E.M. Nelayan, Colonel Tinsely, Lt. Colonels H.H. MacDonald, H.C. Smith, Major L.C.R. Kingdom,

Judge Advocate Lt. Col. J.T. Brock, Chief Prosecutor Mr. L.C. Badham K.C. with Wing Commander T.S. McKay and Major H.F. Dick. Major General Ujima, assisted by Takiz Omae, Lt. Col. Asamu Murayama and six other members of the Japanese Legal Corps, made up the defence.

I was the chief direct witness in this case. The other was documentary evidence. The trial had started on 8th April 1947 and ended on 23rd April. The accused had been found guilty and had been given life imprisonment.

The other trial was of Major-General Akira Hirota, supply commander of field depots of the Japanese 8th Army in New Britain. He was charged with committing war atrocities, in that he, between December 1942 and July 1945 in New Britain, whilst commanding the armed forces of Japan at war with Australia, unlawfully disregarded and failed to discharge his duties as commander to control the conduct of his forces whereby they committed atrocities against the people of Australia and her allies.

In Hirota's case, crimes committed by his subordinates concerned the ill treatment and murder of Chinese POWs, Indians and natives of

New Guinea. He too was found guilty and given a seven-year imprisonment. This time I had an eleven month stay again in Australia and came back.

This ends my brief story of how I eventually got back home after 5 years, which I had lost. It is a miracle to come back alive after passing so many hardships and changes. I have won a big game when many thousands of unfortunate people have failed. I am confident the prayers of my dear wife, mother and sister and other members of my family helped me very much. Moreover, my hope never gave way and the verse of Mr. Bryant has served as a motto for me. Here it is again -

"The lights of smiles shall fill again,
The lids that overflow with tears,
And the weary hours of woe and pain,
Are promises of happier years."

Appendix I
RETURN TO WEWAK, 1970

I NEVER THOUGHT in my lifetime I shall ever be able to re-visit and pay homage to the land of my re-birth. In July 1970, I received a letter from Army Headquarters that I was required to attend the 25th anniversary of Japanese surrender celebrations at Wewak, New Guinea on 13th September 1970 as guest of honour of the Australian armed forces. After having gone through the formalities, I left India on 4th September and landed at Port Moresby on the 7th. I hurriedly visited the place where we used to cremate our dead and offered my prayers for departed Indian souls. I was taken to the places of my interest where I had suffered, along with my friends.

There was a big gathering, people from America, Australia and Japan. The ceremonies lasted for three days consisting of a ceremonial parade, opening of a war memorial, laying of wreaths, several social functions and visits to places of interest. A special plane was chartered for me and Lieutenant-Commander MC Hordern, of the Australian Navy, to fly us to Angoram, the place of my re-birth 25 years ago. We were received at the airport by the Deputy Commissioner and went to the exact spot where M.L. 1347, commanded by (then Lieutenant) Hordern, had berthed and took us to safety and the hospital. We met old natives of the area who recognised me.

After some prayers at the spot, we were entertained by the Deputy Commissioner to lunch and then flew back to Wewak. It gave me the greatest satisfaction of my life to have paid homage to the departed souls of Indian POWs in New Guinea and a visit to the place of my re-birth. I cherish those memories with great pride.

After the functions at Wewak were over, I was given an opportunity to visit my friends in Sydney, Canberra, Melbourne and Perth. It was very thrilling and exciting to meet the old veterans of WW2 who had turned the tide of war in the favour of the Allies in the Kokoda battle and had saved my life from Japanese hands. In Canberra, I was entertained by the Indian High Commissioner, Mr Thomas and also by Colonel Bhandari, Military Adviser to the High Commissioner. I came back to India via Singapore and halted there for two days and re-visited all the places known to me from my WW2 days.

Operation Remembrance

The civil authorities and the Returned Services League (RSL) in Wewak were very moved on hearing my account of the sufferings which my comrades and I had gone through in New Guinea. As a result, they prepared a proposal to construct two more monuments in memory of Indian soldiers who had become martyrs in New Guinea. It was sent to me for my comments, which I promptly did and returned to them. They wanted me to send two stones from my village in Himachal Pradesh to be imbedded in the monuments which were to be constructed at Angoram and Wewak. They also wanted a shroud to veil the monuments, the unveiling of which was to be done by the Indian High Commissioner in Australia on 30th September 1971. The Assistant District Commissioner, Mr Kerry Leen and Mr Denni Bernard, President of the RSL, Wewak were the architects of this project and it was completed on 25th September. The Indian Military and Air Advisor to the High Commission went to New Guinea. The two monuments in New Guinea in memory of Indian soldiers who never returned home were unveiled. It gave me the greatest satisfaction that at least two foreign countries, New Guinea and Australia, recognised the sacrifice of my comrades and constructed monuments in their memory.

Note: Sadly, these monuments were washed away during floods in the Sepik river and have not been rebuilt.

Lt. Marsden Hordern, RANVR and Chint Singh in September 1970 on the bank of Sepik river, where they met for the first time in September 1945

Chint Singh and Lt Marsden Hordern, RANVR, attending "Return to Wewak", Sept 1970, to commemorate 25th Anniversary of Japanese surrender

Chint Singh after laying wreath at cenotaph, Wewak, September 1970,
commemoration of 25th Anniversary of Japanese surrender in WW2

Chint Singh and Lt Marsden Hordern and other officers

Chint Singh in Indian Army Uniform, feeling proud to represent his country at "Return to Wewak" commemoration

With some natives of Papua and New Guinea, September, 1970

Appendix II
OPERATION REMEMBRANCE - 1971

THE FOLLOWING ACCOUNT is given by Kerry Leen, who was the driving force behind 'Operation Remembrance'.

Kerry Leen, Wewak, Assistant Commissioner Sepik Area, New Guinea

BACKGROUND

During the return to Wewak in September of last year, some of us had the rare privilege of listening to the war-time reminiscences of Major Chint Singh, ex 2/12th Frontier Force Regiment, India, and Lieutenant-Commander Tony Marsden Hordern (R.A.N.V.R.) – the circumstances under which they met 26 years before at Angoram on the banks of the mighty Sepik River – some weeks after the official surrender by Lieutenant-General Hataze Adachi, G.O.C. XVIII Japanese Imperial Army to Major-General H.C.H. Robertson, G.O.C., Australian Sixth Division, at Cape Wom on 13th September, at 1015 hours, 1945.

There at Angoram, a fair number of Japanese troops held as

POWs, eleven Indian soldiers, including Jemadar (Lieutenant) Chint Singh – these being the sole survivors of some 3000 Indian troops captured during the fall of Singapore and subsequently shipped by freighters to the Sepik, landing at Wewak on 16th May, at 0700 hours, 1943; other Indian troops captured at Singapore were likewise shipped direct to New Britain – all to be used as a labour force for the Japanese Armed Forces.

Chint states the main causes of annihilation of his countrymen in the Sepik campaign was disease, lack of medical attention, lack of food and mass executions, such as at But Village on the 24th and 25th April 1944 where several hundred of his comrades were shot – several days later some 200 were shot in one day at Boiken Village. They were being used as carriers for the Japanese mass exodus along the coast, attempting to link up with their forces at Hollandia – the American (with No.62 Works Wing, R.A.A.F.) landings at Aitape on 22nd April, set this retreat off – the Japanese dispersed after their failure in the battle of the Driniumor River – over the ranges into the Haprik-Dreikikir areas and back east along the cast to the Wewak/Alexander Range areas; no doubt the unfortunate Indian carriers had become an embarrassment to them. Many Indian POWs, of course, were killed by Allied bombing and strafing raids.

First to reach Angoram after the formal surrender at Cape Wom was an Angau party headed by Lieutenant F.O. Monk with Dr. J.S. Greham, Warrant Officer P.F. Flenberg and some 40 local soldiers – they convinced the Japanese there the surrender was a reality, took over the welfare of Chint and his 10 mates all of whom were ill, half-starved and utterly dejected after their long sufferings. On the arrival of Monk's party, Chint loudly exclaimed, "WE ARE REBORN" taken up in chorus by his mates. Chint explained when in Wewak last September, he and his mates never lost their faith they would be 'reborn' and 'liberated'. Some days after Monk's arrival along came R.A.N.V.R. Fairmile M.L..1347 skippered by Lieutenant Tony Marsden Horden – reinforced by barges from No. 43 Australian Landing Barge Company, headed by Lieutenants K.W. Peterson and A. Galt – aboard one of these barges was big Bob Robson who of recent date forwarded to Denny Barnard (President Wewak RSL Sub-Branch) photographs taken on this historical occasion at Angoram. Incidentally, Bob prior to arriving at Angoram, was at Kairiru Island at the pre-briefing session to Rear Admiral Sato regarding his surrender terms, before Sato surrendered the 27th Japanese Imperial Naval Forces to Red Robbie on 10th September, 1945, aboard Fairmile M.L.805 in Kairiru Strait, skippered by a contemporary of Tony's – one Lieut Sturt, R.A.N.V.R. – with another Fairmile M.L.809 skippered by Lieut Ivan Hogg, R.A.N.V.R. which anchored next to M.L.805.

No. 43 Landing Barge Company took the Japanese and their stretcher cases down river, then along the coast to Cape Wom, where they received treatment before internment at Muschu Island adjacent to Kairiru Island.

Tony Marsden Hordern and the crew of M.L..1346 took Chint to his ten mates along the same route to hospitalisation at Cape Wom, where with medical care and proper diet, they regained their health somewhat. Chint shared a tent with Captain D.H. Bruce (presently Secretary of the RSL Perth W.A.) At a later date Chint's ten mates were placed on an R.A.A.F. aircraft for Rabaul, to testify at Adachi's trial, thence be repatriated to their homeland. It was not to be. Fate decreed with a crooked roll of the die otherwise - the plane crashed into a mountain whilst crossing New Britain- all aboard were killed. Chint still at Cape Wom in shocked solitude, looked askance at fate – he alone of 3000 remained – he alone was to testify at Adachi's trial – he alone returned to Wewak and alone he stood in dignity amongst the 6th Division blokes on 13th September, 1945 at Cape Wom, representing his Government's sacrifice of 3000 of her native sons in the Sepik campaign.

Chint arrived at Wewak on the eve of 11th September. For the return last year, he was met by a Channel Islander, the President of the Wewak RSL. The man responsible for the return, one ex-Sgt. Dennis

Barnard, M.I.D., a veteran of the Normandy landing and European operations. Chint asked Denny to drive him to Waringe Ck, which is on the road to Cape Wom. It was on the banks of this creek many of Chint's comrades had been cremated after dying from the perils of war. As the sun set in the west, this lone man from India silently prayed for the souls of his 3000 mates, then he washed his hands in the waters of Waringe Ck – silently observed by a lone sentry – the Channel Islander.

On 15th September Chint, with Tony Hordern and Denny, travelled by light aircraft to Angoram and walked to the spot on the banks of the Sepik river where M.L..1347 and No. 43 Australian Landing Barge Company, had tied up 25 years before – Chint stood looking at the swirling waters silently praying for his comrades and washed his hands in the waters of the Sepik – standing a little way back was Tony Hordern – no doubt his memories were flickering back along the corridors of time – further back stood the man from the Channel Islands with many native ex-soldiers amongst them, ex-Lance Corporal Ampu (Angau) and ex-Constable Ampulla (Police & Angua) both of whom were in F.O. Monk's party 25 years before on this very spot - in the sunlight on this day – Indian, Australian Channel Islander and local ex-soldiers saw and felt a man's love for his fellowmen and a spiritual blessing.

THE CREATION OF OPERATION REMEMBRANCE

Denny and I had long talks about the fore-going, noting there was no plaque at Cape Wom in commemoration of the sacrifice made by Chint's mates – the impact Waringe Ck and Angoram had made upon us – thus Operation Remembrance was conceived and brought to reality by the Wewak Sub-Branch of the RSL and the Ex-servicemen's Association at Angoram. A memorial would be built at both spots made of sand and stone from all over the Sepik – identical in design – the one at Waringe was titled "MARTYRS MEMORIAL" as Chint had written to us saying, "According to our religious beliefs, a soldier who dies on the battlefield for the cause of freedom and righteousness becomes immortal, and he is respected and given the honour of a Martyr. We therefore believe that all soldiers who died in New Guinea have become immortal". The title of the memorial at Angoram is "WE ARE REBORN".

I will not elaborate on the skulduggery and spivery that went on in trying to find cement in Wewak when there was none in town. As acting District Commissioner during the period of the building of the two memorials, my junior staff in the field received, what was to their minds, odd instructions, e.g. "Please forward as a matter of extreme urgency half copra sack various types of stones from your area (STOP) classify as Geological Specimens (STOP) Place on first aircraft or vehicle, trawler, etc."

There was no resultant stoney silence!! Stones duly arrived by trawler, vehicle and aircraft from all parts of the Sepik, inclusive of Ambunti, Maprik, Aitape, Yangoru, Dagua, But and Boiken (where those dreadful executions took place) Cape Wom, Mission Hill, Waringe Ck and Wewak Hill. We wrote to Chint to send two large stones from his own hearth in India – fortunately Howard Vinning (State Sec. New Guinea RSL) called on Chint en route home from a trip to Europe; Chint sighed happily and gave Howard two stones weighing about 5lbs each for delivery to Wewak – the airfreight from India has kept Chint broke for six months. We do not believe Howard's story that Australian and New Guinea customs wanted to break open the stones, thinking they may have contained Indian hemp or some other aphrodisiac recommended by the Kama Sutra. Howard is still screaming about the cost of the airfreight from Lae to Wewak. One each was placed on each memorial.

Chint had previously approached the Indian Government to present a plaque for placement at Cape Wom in memory of the 3000 Indian soldiers who died in the Sepik campaigns. His efforts came to fruition – the plaque arrived from the Indian High Commissioner, Canberra, with notification that Colonel O.S. Bhandari, Military, Naval and Air Adviser to the High Commissioner would arrive in

Wewak on the 28th September to unveil the plaque at Cape Wom and the memorials at Waringe Ck, and Angoram. Chint sent the Indian National Flag from his regiment to Canberra to be used in the unveilings and this was brought to Wewak by Colonel Bhandari.

The design of the memorials and the working for the plaques was forwarded to Chint for approval – he smartly replied and the actual work of building them got under way exactly 14 days before the 30th and work was completed on the 27th. Bob Becke, Assistant District Commissioner at Angoram received the plans and numerous packages of stones by courtesy of aerial Tour Manager, Maurice Imray – the pilots, used to queer and odd cargo consignments, looked askance at stones going to Angoram and stones from Angoram to Wewak (for Waringe Ck) on the return flights.

Bob was greatly assisted by Don Bosgard of Angoram, who looks after the ex-servicemen's needs down there and also Mr. Hilmar Fevang, a Norwegian ex-serviceman, employed by Public Works who with the ex-servicemen cleared the ground and built the memorial on the approximate spot where 26 years ago M.L..1347 tied up with the barges from No.43 Australian Landing Barge Company, where Chint prayed and washed his hands on the 15th September last year, watched by Tony Hordern, Denny Barnard and the ex-servicemen.

Meanwhile in Wewak, Denny Barnard, Noel Butler, Lloyd Yelland, Bill Rendall and some ex-servicemen and myself as 'beer joey' got busy at Waringe Ck. The design of both memorials is identical. ie. a 6" by 4" cement base with the stones set in and a cement reinforced upright in the centre some 3" thick some 5' 6" in height with the plaques placed near the top.

Angoram Plaque

"WE ARE REBORN" Lt. Chint Singh.

"ON THIS SPOT ON THE 30-9-45 LT.HORDEN (RANVR) WITH CRSM OF VESSEL ML.1347 ANCHORED THEN EVACUATED

US TO COMFORT AND SAFETY AFTER LT. MONK AND HIS LOCAL SOLDIERS HAD FOUND AND FED US – 11 SOULS OF THE INDIAN ARMY ONLY SURVIVORS FROM JAPANESE CAPTIVITY DURING WAR YEARS 1943-1945.

Wewak. RSL.

Waringe Ck Plaque.

"MARTYRS MEMORIAL"

IT WAS HERE ON THE BANKS OF WARINGE CK DURING WORLD WAR II INDIAN SOLDIERS (POWs) CREMATED THEIR FELLOWMEN WHO DIED FROM THE PERILS OF WAR.

Best Memory. Wewak. RSL.

A cement base was made to the rear of the memorial at Cape Wom to receive the plaque from the Indian government. It reads as follows:

"IN MEMORY OF 3000 INDIAN SOLDIERS WHO DURING WORLD WAR II AS PRISONERS OF WAR IN THIS COUNTRY IN JAPANESE CAPTIVITY MADE THE SUPREME SACRIFICE OF THEIR LIVES AND ESTABLISHED A UNIQUE EXAMPLE OF EXTREME DEVOTION TO DUTY AND LOYALTY FOR THE CAUSE OF RIGHTEOUSNESS AND PEACE IN THE WORLD.

MAY GOD BLESS THEM"

The ceremonies

Colonel O.S. Bhandari arrived at Wewak on the 28th, met by Colonel Lloyd, OBE, MC, Commanding Officer, No.2 Pacific Islands Regiment. Moem Barracks would be host to Col. Bhandari during his 3 day stay. Denny Barnard and myself were at the airport to meet him. He was accompanied by his aide, 2nd Lieutenant Thomas Niaga, (ex Ambunti) from No. 1 P.I.R. Murray Barracks, Port Moresby. Next to arrive was Howard Vinning, accompanied by robust Ossie Osborne (Deputy State President). State President John Hughes could not make it owing to ill-health.

The arrangements were we would all proceed to Angoram by aircraft on the morrow, overnighting so we would be at the memorial at dawn officially, timed to be 5.50am EST. Colonel Lloyd gave wonderful assistance. A bugler, a piper, two army chaplains, an adjutant and a photographer accompanied him. Denny, myself, Don Coffey and wife, Ossie and Howard, an ABC representative, a representative from Radio Wewak, all converge on Angoram. Here 64 ex-servicemen were lined up at the parking bay to pay homage to Colonel O.S. Bhandari. Included amongst them was a widow holding her late husband's shirt on a coat hanger, with his service medals attached to it. The colonel inspected this guard of honour and spoke to most of them individually, including the widow. In charge of this old veteran guard of honour was ex-Sergeant- Major Maiyak. All had met Chint and Tony on 15th September 1970 on their visit to Angoram.

The president of the Angoram's Ex-servicemen Association then invited us all to their clubhouse for drinks. His name was ex-Sergeant Kaman-Iambui. He made a speech of welcome in Pidgin-English to Colonel Bhandari and presented him with two carvings, one for Chint and one for himself. The colonel suitably replied in English and said inter alia "There is an unbreakable bond between this country of yours and India – we are one people." Ossie Osborne then commenced his speech. Many beers later, long after the sun had set, Ossie finished his speech and enquired of the ex-servicemen if they had an alarm clock to wake them up for the dawn service. President Kaman-Iamhul the aged veteran replied, "Maski long clock mipela e got kukuruak i savvy cri out three pella time-numba three im i cri mi get up' (Never mind the clock we have a rooster who cries out 3 times, the third time, it is time to get up).

We adjourned to the Angoram Hotel where we were overnighting, where my hosts Geoff King and wife looked after all in a splendid manner, making our stay a memorable one. At 5am, on the morning of the 30th, a loud commotion awoke everyone. It so happened the good Colonel Bhandari arose first, to awake the rest of us and in so doing, locked himself out of his room; several hotel employees ranging from the cook to the barboy were fiercely attacking his door with chisels and hammers. Ossie could be heard practicing another speech as he shaved!

I shared a room with Denny Barnard. As we were about to depart our room for the dawn service, the conversation went as follows:

Denny: Have you got the camera?

Self: Yes.

Denny: The tape recorder?

Self: Yes

Denny: Have you got the Indian Flag?

Self: Yes.

Denny: What about the water from Waringe Ck?

Self: I have it.

Denny: Have you the prayer to be read out for the blessing?

Self: In my pocket.

Denny: What about the wreaths?

Self: The ex-servicemen have theirs – Geoff King is taking down yours, Colonel Lloyd's and Bhandari's.

Denny: Good. Now where's the torch?

Self: There on the chair. You carry it – I can't carry anymore; I look like a bloody old Bro-wery horse now with all its trappings and bridles, etc.

Denny: O.K. let's go, incidentally give me a cigarette and a light. I left mine in the dining room last night.

Self: (Censored – unprintable!!!)

It was quite dark at the memorial site – except for the two kerosene burners placed either side of the memorial – the Indian flag was then placed over the memorial and the canister of water from Waringe Ck placed on the base where the Sepik River was added. The entire population of Angoram had turned out - numbering some 160, inclusive of the 64 ex-servicemen (the rooster had obviously cried out on time) plus the widow again holding her later husband's shirt with his service medals attached to it. Directly in front of the memorial stood Denny Barnard; Colonel Lloyd; Colonel Bhandari and the president of the Angoram ex-servicemen's association, the aged ex-Sgt-Kaman-Iambul. In the far-right-hand corner of the gravel square stood the No. 2 P.I.R. Piper, Warrant Officer Tiamoua; in the opposite corner No. 2 P.I.R. Bugler, Sergeant Awini – to the rear of the memorial and facing it stood Colonel Bhandari's aide, 2nd Lieutenant Thomas Niaga. The ex-servicemen were three deep to the rear of those immediately in front of the memorial.

It was now a few minutes to dawn – silence, except for the awakening chatter of small birds above in the trees – the only movement was the flickering flames from the two burners. One could just discern the mist on the waters of the Sepik – when the mellow haunting notes of The Last Post echoed out, heralding the 9, 125th dawn since F.O. Monk and party walked into this area – Chint in far-away India would be at prayers at this very moment (he had been advised by radio that dawn was 5.50 EST) Tony Hordern in Sydney was also aware – both had been sent the sequence of events for this dawn service. Dawn subtly broke on cue, as it were, on the final notes of The Last Post – silence for a few seconds, even from the small birds, no doubt intrigued by such a strange ritual in their sanctuary – then softly began the elegiac notes of The Lament from the piper as the mist unfurled back along the river revealing the delicate pink sky of this dawn; the Lament softly continued. Chaplain Ossie Dale (No. 2 P.I.R) led us all in the opening prayers, then Mr. Kyrill Bland of the Seventh Day Adventist Mission commenced the prayer for the blessing of the memorial and flag, which was as follows:

"O Heavenly Father – we stand at Angoram before You at dawn on the birth of this 30th day of September 1971 to remember those eleven Indian soldiers who were rescued from the perils of war on this spot

26 years ago today and to pray for the soul of all those Indian Martyrs who died for their country's cause during the war years of World War II. It is then fitting that this flag from their homeland should cover their memorial. O Heavenly Father, as one of your servants on earth here at Angoram, I call upon you to be with me in blessing this flag of India and sacred memorial."

Mr. Bland then sprinkled the mixed waters of Waringe Ck and the Sepik River over the national flag of India and the memorial. Colonel Bhandari then stepped forward and unveiled the memorial by folding the national flag of India over the top to be received by his Aide 2nd-Lieutenant Thomas Niaga who folded the flag and placed it under his right arm, then stood to attention: the Colonel stood upright, saluted and stepped back. The revealed plaque carried its own message for posterity – ever to be jealously guarded against vandalism by the multi-racial population of Angoram, now and in the future. Angoram has now entered into history.

Whilst the Lament continued, Denny Barnard recited Laurence Binyon's immortal Valediction "They shall grow not old…". It was my humble honour to then follow with the translation in Pidgin-English. The laying of the wreaths commenced with Barnard, Colonel Bhandari, Colonel Lloyd and the aged ex-Sgt. Kaman-Iamiul. The man from the Channel Islands then in an emotional voice, read out Major Chint Singh's letter of the day. All then joined Chaplain Austin Crapp, No.2 P.I.R., in the Lord's Prayer.

The Lament ceased. A few moments of silence and meditation, broken only by the excited chatter of the small birds, then the echo in the distance of the crowing of a rooster. Odd perhaps, but drowned by the beautiful notes of reveille played by Sgt. Awini. 'Tis done – the first stage of Operation Remembrance – a simple ceremony, touching, spiritual, racial companionship, a bond between countries. Each with his own thoughts and memories. Some thinking of Chint, Tony, Monk, Peterson, Galt, Robson, the ex-servicemen? Thinking of their mates lost in a war not of their making. Yet here homage has been paid. Prayers have been sincerely spoken – a moving, deeply spiritual experience – the fellowship of men with a capital M regardless of race or creed.

As we stood around, before moving off, THE rooster came out of the undergrowth with sprightly, staccato steps, flicking its head from side to side, eyes furtively taking in all, poised on one leg, with the other claw clenched, viewed the scene; in imagery. Similar to an old time Mississippi river boat gambler wearing a guilt complex owing to five aces being clenched in his fist!! Unable to assess events, it did a smart reverse and ran into the scrub: "I'm I clock bilong mipela' rasped the aged President of the Angoram Ex-servicemen's Association – my humble opinion is the Swiss have a lot to learn regarding alarm clocks that personally check on who got out of bed and who did not!!

All adjourned to the Angoram Hotel for a gunfire breakfast – rum, coffee, bacon and eggs. Geoff King and his wife were terrific in all aspects. I spoke to Warrant Officer Tiamoua and complimented him on the playing of the Lament.

"Ah, Mr. Leen eye bilong me I run na mi praid mi shortwind too much". (I had tears in my eyes and was afraid that my wind would not hold out in playing The Lament). On speaking to Sgt. Awini – 'Mi tink long ol lapun'.

One-tok soldier im I stand up: na dispel meri one taim shirt na medal bilong man bilong im – na one-taim ol man I die long fight – mi haramas tru, Mr Leen." This brought a bloody great lump to my throat – as his words were "I thought of all those old ex-servicemen standing there at attention and the widow with her husband's shirt with his medals on it and all the men who died in the war – I was proud to play The Last Post and Reveille, Mr. Leen".

Snatches of conversation overhead at breakfast at the Angoram pub… "Jesus, it was a touching show"… "Yeah.. I'll pay the Piper"… "True.. But Sgt. Awini sure can blow a sweet horn"… "Hey, Ossie never got to making a speech"… "Quiet.. or he'll start now you silly bastard"… "well without the P.I.R., it would not have been the show it was"... "That's right I'll pay the P.I.R."... "It's a beaut memorial... and fancy having a stone from India set in it"... "Yeah, ask Howard Vinning about that one"... "T'was a good show the ex-servicemen put on last night"... "Yeah... Ossie told them so far an hour in his speech"... "Do you reckon Chint and Tony were up?... "I'll give you 100 to nothing they were"... "What time would it have been in India?... "Buggered if I know, ask Colonel Bhandari"... Not a bad bike Bhandari"... "Yeah.. but he does not have to chop doors down at dawn"... "Kerry did you tape everything?" All except that roster's footsteps.. oli I callin Alarm!!! ... "The padres did a good job"... "Yeah, three and no professional jealousy"... "I hope the photographs come out O.K."... "Hey Howard tell us about the Customs wanting to unscrew your stones"... "What's the score this afternoon? "Cape Wom at 5.15 – then Waringe at sunset"... "I'll have a run".

We took our farewells from the good people of Angoram and travelled by several planes from Aerial Tours, back to Wewak. The inevitable happens. As usual, I have more trappings than the proverbial bravery horse, camera, tape-recorder, bottle of Sepik river water for the ceremony at Waringe, my overnight bag, so I entrust the Indian Flag to Denny, who only has his overnight bag. It was a wonder I wasn't carrying that too! What happens? Half way to Wewak he remembers he left the flag at the pub!! No more aircraft to call at Angoram that day... fortunately our good friend Maurice Imray to the rescue again.. he diverted a plane into Angoram at 2.30 p.m. but the weather was doubtful. The Channel Islander really did some sweating as he waited at Bran airstrip. The flag arrived at 3 pm.

At 5.15pm we all arrived at the 6th Div Memorial at Cape Wom. Local ex-servicemen (all members of the Wewak RSL) were well represented. The ceremony was simple: The Last Post, Prayers, The unveiling of the Indian plaque, a speech by Colonel Bhindari, myself in reply as acting District Commissioner, Prayers then a few seconds mediation followed by Reveille. India is represented for prosperity at Cape Wom.

As the sun began to set, we moved off to Waringe Creek on the Dagua Road. The No. 2 P.I.R. piper stood on the western banks of the creek, exactly where Chint prayed last September; a few yards to his left stood the bugler. The memorial, by administrative necessity, is built on the eastern bank. This ceremony followed the pattern of the dawn service at Angoram. Rev. Fr. Ruiter of the Catholic Mission conducted the Blessing, with waters from the Sepik and Waringe. His prayer exactly the same as spoken by Mr. Kyrill Bland at Angoram. Where at Angoram at dawn, it was darkness, mist, subtle light, the chatter of small birds, here it was stillness with the last rays of sunlight angling down through the palms, in a farewell salute as it were. The first rays and the last of this day had shone on two memorials of memory.. yet will continue to shine on them in perpetual benediction as they represent the souls of 3000 sons of India. These 3000 souls, Martyrs from India, owe a deep debt to the man who was the last to survive at Cape Wom in 1945. Through his sincerity, dignity and personality, he inspired us in Wewak to build these two memorials and activate his government into providing the bronze plaque at Cape Wom in commemoration of the Fallen from India. As Colonel O.S. Bhandari said to the Sepik ex-servicemen, "There is an unbreakable bond between our countries." The man alone, who forged that bond, who inspired us all – Major Chint Singh.

THEN THERE WAS A BALL –YES!.. AND OSSIE MADE A SPEECH

The night of 30th September, the committee Wewak festivities again excelled themselves (Bunny Girls – unfortunately, all married does!!) Drinks, supper, music. Colonel Bhandari was introduced to all those good people of Wewak who had assisted so much in the return to Wewak celebrations, then RSL certificates were issued to 19 persons who greatly assisted the return to Wewak activities in the previous September. Ossie was in his element, made a speech outlining the difficulty in obtaining such a certificate from the RSL and the unique occasion such as this one where 19 such certificates were granted. Each was presented by Colonel Bhandari – Ossie's long speech was bearable owing to such pleasurable diversions as outlined above.

Colonel Bhandari departed Wewak two days later, taking with him the Indian National Flag, which will be sent over to Chint in India by the Indian High Commission, Canberra.

(Kerry Leen).

DRAFT RADIO SCRIPT FOR 9AJ WEWAK - 19TH OCTOBER 1945

INTRODUCING JEMADAR CHINT Singh of 2/12 Frontier Force Regt. Hometown in Punjab, India. He was rescued from the Japanese with ten other Indians at Angoram, Sepik Area, on 30th September 1945.

1. What is your military service?

   Chint Singh: Just ten years. I served on India's north-west frontier and then in Malaya against Japanese.

2. What happened to you after Singapore fell?

   Chint Singh: Singapore fell on 15th Feb 1942. Indians were kept separate from the Australian and the British. Japs started a movement called the Indian National Army. There were certain officers and men who joined it, but most of them had run away from the field and were on the black list. They tortured the Indians and killed some of them. The Japs threatened that they would take us to the Solomon and Burma fronts and keep us under heavy bombardments of the allies and so they did. They organised unwilling soldiers into parties and sent them overseas. We, about 3000, were taken to New Guinea, out of which 11 of us are survivors today.

3. Describe your working conditions at Wewak?

Chint Singh: We stayed 3 months in the swamp near Wom and had to come to Wewak aerodrome early in the morning and back about 6 or 7pm. We were given no holiday, or time for bathing, washing and cooking. Then we shifted towards Wewak, distance about 2 miles and made huts in the swamp. We were kept in quite unhealthy surroundings. The sick men suffering from beri-beri, tropical ulcers and malaria were forced to work on the aerodromes and harbours for days and nights continuously. Jap Colonel in charge of the parties used to keep time that was 34 minutes to cover the distance of two miles. About 20% could not do this and were daily beaten. Before we started work, the Japs also began to count us. This sometimes took two hours while they were making up their minds what to do with us. Many times we had to stand for hours in the sun while Japs could not decide.

4. What were your food supplies like?

Chint Singh: Food was so poor in quantity and quality that in the first two months, 200 men suffered from beri-beri out of the 539 in my party. One day, a coolie asked me why Indians did not steal and advised me to steal, otherwise all of us would die of starvation. He had some stolen sugar with him, which I exchanged with my new shorts and thanked him. The Indian officers organised the men into small parties to steal food, medicine and other requirements. During the day, we watched the dumps and in the night we had to run four or five miles carrying our loads as well as we could. Our tactics for stealing and robbing from the Japs became so crafty that in the presence of two of three sentries, we could steal easily. Whenever we could find their cooking pots full of any cooked food, we used to run away with that into the bush. One day, a sentry caught four of our men with fish boxes and called for others to help. In the meantime, one of the boys hit him on his head with the box. The sentry fell unconscious and they succeeded in getting away. They killed many of our men while stealing. They tried to stop stealing by religious punishments such as cutting the hair of the Sikh, forcing tobacco into their mouths, burning their long beards and moustaches, cutting the sacred hair of Hindus and using our Bibles for smoking tobacco. As the Allies harassed and paralysed the Japs with their new machines and weapons, similarly we astonished them with our new methods of stealing and sabotage, though it cost us many lives.

5. Did the Japanese give your sick adequate medical treatment?

Chint Singh: ... once we sent our 15 serious cases to their big hospital at Moem, where within ten days, ten died. They were not attended by any Jap doctor and only once a day were given little rice. Generally, all cases of tropical ulcers used to get maggots in their wounds and sometimes the boys requested, 'sir, cut our throats with a knife or something' and some were ready to go to their graves alive. Our medical officers, who were about 45-years-old and could not carry big loads, were tortured more than the other men. Two died and one is safe in Australia.

6. I believe that you took a copy of international law to the Japs. What did they say?

Chint Singh: Yes, I still keep that copy with me and once I showed it to Colonel Thakana and told him, 'Look here, it is signed by your government and you should abide by it'. He howled and said, 'I do not take any notice of rules and regulations'.

7. Often they tried to make you go against British. What propaganda did they use?

Chint Singh: They forced us to go against the British by threats and torture. They used to say that they were going to capture New Delhi and will take us to India. They posted propaganda sheets in the area where we used to live and some of them I will read to you –

a. 15th July 1943 - 20,000 Indians in Malaya and Singapore are ready to fight the English, you must cooperate with them otherwise suffer more than the present time.

b. 23rd July 1943 – Japanese have occupied Bengal and Subhash Bose has come from Germany to Singapore and has taken command of the Indian Army.

c. 13th August 1943 – In India there are many internal revolutions and within a short time, India will be free. Any Indian desirous to go to Singapore should report to his commander and will be sent by air.

8. Did the Japs get any volunteers?

Chint Singh: No

9. Did you witness any of the Allied raids on Wewak?

Chint Singh: It was the 17th August 1943 when we were working in the Wewak aerodrome. There was a sudden attack of bombers at about 8.30am. It was so sudden that the Japs could not save a single aeroplane on the ground. The bombers were counting and hitting the aircraft and guns. About 200 planes were burnt on the ground. Eight of our men were wounded.

We used to tremble with fear that the 'flying fortresses' might start unleashing their cargo on us, but when the bombs used to fall on Wewak Point, then we used to enjoy the sight and count bombs. Double bodied fighters used to engage from 10 to 15 Japs fighters…Many times I saw Jap planes coming down in pairs after one long burst of fire.

10. Were any of your men hit?

Chint Singh: Yes, we lost about 15 men and an equal number were wounded.

11. How did the Jap Colonel treat your wounded men?

Chint Singh: … One day, he took the wounded men in a truck from the aerodrome to our huts. On the way when the wounded were crying in pain, he stopped his truck and threw dust on their faces and said: 'this is the treatment you deserve'.

12. When you made long treks carrying supplies for the Japanese, what happened to your very sick personnel who were left behind?

Chint Singh: The Japs never cared for our very sick patients who could not walk and left them in the jungle helpless. Once a sergeant who came back to carry his sick brother found that the Japs had killed all the patients, who were about 16 in number. I think all the men who were left on the way met the same fate.

13. When the position became hopeless for them on the coast, the Japs made you go inland. Where did you go?

Chint Singh: We marched to the Maprik area and then to the far south in the hills.

14. How long did it take?

Chint Singh: We marched on the 29th Sept 1944 and reached the destination on 16th Dec 1944. We made a journey of about

1000 miles through some of the worst country in the world. We went to and fro carrying our own sac-sac and Jap packages.

15. What loads were you carrying?

Chint Singh: There were 480 packages, not less that 80lbs each and 300 bags of rice and some salt, sugar, fish and ammunition carried by 241 Indians. Whenever we made any request for salt or anything, their shrewd reply was 'send a wireless message to Roosevelt and Churchill and get it from them'. One officer, Jem Harnam Singh of 6/14 Punjab Regt was beheaded because they found one bottle of quinine with him.

16. How many Indians were there initially in your party?

Chint Singh: 539 – now there are seven survivors. (The other four Indians rescued were from other parties).

Q: What was the reason for one of your officers taking his own life?

Chint Singh: Jem Shivdayal of 6/14 Punjab Regt suffered from beri-beri and could not walk and carry his own sac-sac so was severely beaten until he fell down in the swamp. He could not bear it, picked up a rifle off the guard and shot himself. There were two other soldiers who hung themselves and thus rid themselves of Japanese tortures for ever.

Q: What happened to one of your comrades at Kar Kar Village?

Chint Singh: Sepoy Ram Singh of 6/14 Punjab Regt was tied to a tree by the Japanese Lt. Murai, who ordered all the Japs to strike him hard on his face and head in turns and the process was continued for 24 hours. On the following day, they kicked him and left him lying in the hot sun till the evening. One of the Jap sergeants bayoneted him and buried him half dead. He was a strong man and was still alive when the soil was thrown over his head.

Q: What was his crime?

Chint Singh: He had done a great crime!! He had stolen four lemons from the Mission garden because they cure beri beri.

Q: What other instances do you know of killing Indians from other parties?

Chint Singh: Well, there are hundreds and thousands of instances of their savagery and cannibalism, of which the world would not believe. Once in the month of June 1944, a party of Gurkhas and 300 men of the 18th Indian party were machine gunned and bayoneted at But. One of the Gurkhas signalled the allied aircraft and was caught by the Japs. One medical sergeant who escaped told me a miserable story of 300 Indians killed and shot that day.

Q: How did you get on with the natives?

Chint Singh: We were strictly forbidden to talk to them and for this reason only, they shot Capt Hanover, commander of 18th party. The Japs spread propaganda to the natives that these Indians were very dangerous and that they had bombed the natives' houses and villages. But this propaganda turned to our advantage. Later, when the Japs began to retreat to the Sepik, the natives began to think 'in future these Indians will come and govern us'. One of the natives one day said to a group of Kanakas 'Gwim something belong kai kai hidden,' and told me, "white masta and you Indian plenty good, Jap no good, givim me pella nothing, white masta givim me pella knife lap lap and tobacco'. There were certain villages where the natives were very bad. They killed our men and handed over the escaped soldiers to Japs.

Q: Did you see any allied pilots taken by the Japs?

Chint Singh: Yes. I had seen them inside the barbed wire, with two sentries standing over them. They were not allowed to go out. There was one Major amongst them who was allowed to go out to clean the cooking pots and fetch water for them. They were about 40 when we left for Hollandia on 13th April 1944. In the month of May, when we came back, we did not find them. Most probably, the Japs would have shot them. They were very weak; the Japs used to throw boiled rice to them on the ground. They requested to work on the harbour, but they were not permitted to do so. Japs were suspicious that they would signal to the bombers.

Q: Do you know anything of the fate of the 26th Indian Party?

Chint Singh: This party was used to take rations and ammunition to the Japs from But to Aitape side. 19 Indians of this party were eaten by the Japs. The natives told the Indians about it and then Jemadar Mohommet Latif, who is still with me (the only survivor of this entire party) saw the human flesh being cooked in the Japanese cookhouse. The Indians inquired about their lost men and were told that they had run away. The natives also protested against it.

Appendix IV
THE EVIDENCE

The following affidavit of Chint Singh has been sourced from the Australian War Memorial. (Record: AWM54 1010/4/31)

I, CHINT SINGH, of 12 Frontier Force Regiment Indian Army, make oath and say as follows:-

1. I am a Subedar in 12 Frontier Force Regiment and I am at present on the Staff of the Tactical and Administrative School Dera Dun in India. My parent unit is still 12 Frontier Force Regiment of the Indian Army.

2. I was taken a prisoner of war by the Japanese Army at the capitulation of Singapore on the 15th day of February 1942.

3. I remained in and around Singapore until the 5th day of May 1943. During this time, the Japanese formed units known as 16, 17, 18, 19 and 26 Indian Working Parties. These units were composed solely of Indian Prisoners of War and included officers and other ranks.

4. I became a member of 19 Indian Working Party and on the

5th day of May 1943, 16, 17, 18 and 19 Indian Working Parties embarked on two Japanese Transports at Singapore and disembarked at WEWAK in New Guinea on the 16th day of May 1943. 26 Indian Working Party arrived at Wewak about a month later.

5. All the Indian Working Parties remained in New Guinea until the capitulation by the Japanese. The total strength of all Indian Working Parties at the date of formation was about three thousand officers and men.

6. On arrival in Wewak, all working parties were under the command of Colonel TAKANO. Each individual party had its own commander. Col TAKANO remained in command of all Indian Working Parties until the end of December 1943.

7. On arrival, all members of the 5 parties were compelled to erect their own living and sleeping quarters. They were constructed with grass and were totally inadequate, as they did not prevent the rain from coming in. The location of the quarters was five miles from Wewak Point and it was situated in a swamp. On one side was the sea and on the other side was a small creek. When the creek flooded, the water from it surrounded and entered our huts. At this time and for about two months while we remained at this location, it rained practically every day and the water from the creek frequently entered our huts. As a result, we usually slept in water. There were no sanitary conveniences at this camp at all and the condition of the camp increased the incidence of sickness.

8. The selection of the location was made by Col TAKANO and he personally supervised the erection of the quarters. The erection of the huts occupied a day and Col TAKANO was present on about two occasions. He urged the Japanese officers and guards to compel us to hurry with the work.

9. The following day, all working parties, with the exception of 26 Indian Working Party, marched out on fatigues to Wewak Point, a distance of five miles. On this occasion and every day thereafter, Col TAKANO supervised the march from the camp to the harbour at Wewak Point from the highest portion of ground in the area.

10. In July 1943, the location of the camp was moved to a place about 2 miles from Wewak Point. At this time, many Indians had become weak and sick through lack of food, bad conditions under which we were living and the long hours and heavy nature of work. The five-mile march to the place of work had also weakened the health of the men.

11. Col TAKANO then gave orders to the Japanese Guards that all Indians were to march from the new camp to Wewak Point in a period of thirty-four minutes. Many Indians, through weakness and ill health, were unable to make the journey in the time allowed and they were frequently beaten by the Japanese guards and often in the presence of Col TAKANO. Captain KISHA SINGH of 18 Indian Working Party, Captain RAGHWAN, a medical officer of 17 Indian Working Party and some other Indian officers, including myself, approached Col TAKANO who was at that time supervising work on the harbour. Captain RAGHWAN told Col TAKANO that the sick Indians could not cover the distance from the camp in thirty-four minutes. Col TAKANO refused to listen and said, 'Go away'.

12. After the interview with Col TAKANO as referred to in para 11 of this affidavit, more Indians became sick. This further sickness was brought about by the bad condition of the camp site. We were continually living on ground covered with water and it was very swampy. On one side of this camp was a creek which continually flooded into the camp area and at high tide, the sea also flooded the area.

13. There were no sanitary conveniences of any nature at all and in consequence, the camp became very filthy and this also created ill health. At this time also many Indians had contracted tropical ulcers and no action was taken to give sick Indians any medical treatment at all. In all, there were about ten Indian medical officers with the various working parties, but they were made to work on fatigues and they were not given any time to attend to the sick or allowed any medicines to treat the sick.

14. In July 1943 Col TAKANO beat sick Indian himself. At this time we were working at the harbour building a small road. Col TAKANO selected from this group Sepoys SOHNU, JAIRAN and SANTRAN and beat them with a stick about 4 feet long and three inches thick. He said to them, "Why are you working so slowly?" They did not answer because they did not understand what he was saying. He struck each Indian three or four blows on their backs. He also reprimanded the Japanese Guards because they did not force the Indians to work hard. The three sepoys named above were sick. They were suffering from beri-beri.

15. In July 1943, there were about twenty Indians sick in camp. These Indians belonged to 19 Indian Working Party. I was also sick in camp at that time. I was suffering from dysentery. Col. TAKANO came into the camp and ordered all sick men to parade. He then felt the foreheads of every sick man and if a man's forehead was hot, he ordered the guards to give them light duties in the camp. The other men he slapped on the face and ordered to be taken by the guard to work. Two or three of the men were so sick that they were not able to reach the place of work at the harbour. They were beaten by the guards till they were unconscious and they were left on the road. Sick parades as described above were held by Col TAKANO at least twice each week.

16. About the end of July 1943, all senior officers of all Indian working parties signed a petition. The petition was in English and was written out by Captain Nirpal Chand. The petition asked for better food, medicines, medical attention, short working hours and a rest day each week. It also requested that prisoners of war be treated according to International Law, that officers should not be made to work and that Indian medical officers should be allowed to treat their own sick and not made to go on fatigues. In addition, it was also requested that our camp be marked with identifying signs so that Allied airmen would not bomb it. I went with the senior Indian officer to Col TAKANO and acted as interpreter. Col TAKANO could speak English slightly. He had his own interpreter there also, but this interpreter spoke English badly. The petition had been sent to Col TAKANO through Capt IZUMI, the officer commanding 19 Indian Working Party. Col TAKANO came into our camp area and he paraded all the Indian officers who had signed the petition. He was very angry and said to us through the Interpreter "You are traitors of Asia and India". "You have surrendered unconditionally to the Japanese Forces and you should not expect such treatment". "You must do the work you are ordered to do". On this occasion L/Cpl FUKAI acted as the Japanese Interpreter. In addition to the Japanese interpreter, all the Japanese guard officers were present and Col TAKANO said to them "You must not give prisoners opportunities to make requests such as this" and "You must see that they work very hard".

17. In August 1943, we were working on the airstrip at Wewak and Allied aeroplanes bombed the area. This was the first big air raid and about five or six Indians were killed and about thirteen were wounded. The wounded men were brought to camp by Col TAKANO in a big truck and the Indians were

crying out in pain. Col TAKANO picked up handfuls of sand from the beach and threw it at the Indians in anger. He said in broken English, "Why are you crying? This is not my fault. It is Roosevelt and Churchill." They were taken out of the truck and placed on the beach. The Japanese medical officer gave the Indian medical officers some bandages and medical necessities, but the quantity was not nearly sufficient. After a few days, the wounds of the Indians became infected and they all died within a short time thereafter.

18. In August 1943, all senior officers made another similar request to that contained in paragraph 16 of this my affidavit. This request was made to every guard commander of every Indian Working Party. The guard commander of my party, Capt IZUMI, said that Col TAKANO had refused this request before and he could do nothing about it. The senior Indian officers then agreed that all parties should go on a hunger strike. All officers and ranks agreed to refuse food until our requests were heard.

19. All officers and other ranks in 19 Indian Working Party refused breakfast next morning and nothing was cooked for the midday meal. Capt IZUMI and other Japanese guards made enquiries as to our reason for refusing to eat. He then called all the officers together and said, "Why don't you eat". He made some threats to kill certain men and to shoot others and accused us all of causing revolt. Capt NIRPAL CHAND was the spokesman and he said, "We will go without food and die if necessary unless our requests are heard". Capt IZUMI said he would go to Col TAKANO. Col TAKANO came to us and told all the officers that we must eat. NIRPAL CHAND said that we would not eat until our requests were heard. Col TAKANO said to us and to our Japanese Guards "Alright take them to work and I will go to the Army Commander and after his sanction I will kill everybody." We went to work and some Indians could not

continue to work through lack of food. In the afternoon Col TAKANO came and paraded all the officers and said, "Your request will be heard. We admit that you are prisoners of war but cannot put any sign on your camp to show that it is a prisoner of war camp. That would be a disgrace to the Japanese Army". He then ordered the guards to take us back to the camp and food and eat.

20. Conditions improved slightly for about six days and then the ill treatment commenced again.

21. In about July and August 1943 Col TAKANO caused a noticed board to be erected in our camp and he put notices demanding us to join the Indian National Army. These notices said, among other things, that if any man joined the Indian National Army, he would not be made to work and would be sent back to Singapore by air. The Japanese guards also tried to persuade the men to join the Indian National Army, but they all refused. The guards told us that about twenty thousand Indian were co-operating with Japanese in Singapore and were working for the independence of India. They also told us that if we agreed to serve, we would be well treated otherwise we would be treated as traitors and the treatment you are receiving at present will continue.

22. During the whole period, Col TAKANO was in charge of the Indian Working Parties, the food rations of sick Indians were reduced. We asked the Japanese guards why this was done and they said they were orders of Col TAKANO. There were no hospital arrangements for the sick and at numerous times we were compelled to work on the aeroplane strip, to unload from ship, stores, ammunition, petrol, and other military equipment. Col TAKANO was always aware of the work we were doing here and he repeatedly watched us to work and very frequently called out to us to work more quickly.

23. Up to December 1943, when Col TAKANO relinquished his command, about four hundred men had died from ill treatment, lack of food, heavy work and long hours of work, lack of medical necessities and lack of medical treatment. In addition to the four hundred men who died, about three hundred had become almost permanently disabled through tropical ulcers and sickness.

24. Col TAKANO is a man aged over 50 years. He is medium in height, about 5 feet 6 inches. He is a thin man and quick in his actions. He does not wear spectacles and has sharp features.

25. Col IWIKIRI assumed command after Col TAKANO relinquished command in December 1943. Col IWIKIRI did not appear on parades and we saw very little of him. Col IWIKIRI died in Rabaul, but I do not know the date of his death.

Sworn by the above-named deponent at Melbourne

In the State of Victoria, this 19th day of June, One thousand nine hundred and forty-seven.

EPILOGUE

AFTER COMPLETING HIS duty with the 6th Australian Division Headquarters in New Guinea to assist in the War Crimes Board of Inquiry (15th Oct'45 to 16th Jan'46), with the Headquarters 8th Military District Rabaul (10th March'47 to 5th May'47) as witness at the Australian War Crime Commission, and with the Army Headquarters, in Melbourne (21st May'47 to 12th June'47) to assist in the investigation of two cases of atrocities by the Japanese war criminals, Chint Singh returned to India. By the time he returned to India, the 2/12 Frontier Force Regiment in which he was enlisted went to Pakistan after India's independence on 15th August, 1947. As some of the old Frontier Force companies were amalgamated with the Dogra Regiment, he received a commission in 2nd Dogra Regiment in 1947. He served predominantly as a training officer at various defence institutes. Following are his appointments until he retired from defence service in 1974:

> 1948 – 1950: Instructor at Infantry School, Mhow, in the state of Madhya Pradesh

1950 – 1958: 2nd Dogra Regiment, served at various locations and different roles (Company Commander, Quartermaster, Training officer and Adjutant)

1958 – 1960: General Staff Officer, at Headquarters Eastern Command, Lucknow, in the state of Uttar Pradesh

1961 – 1966: Adjutant, Training Major and In-charge Administration, at Army Cadet

College, Nowgong, in the state of Madhya Pradesh and later Pune, in the state of Maharashtra

1966 – 1967: Instructor, Tactical Wing and Adjutant, at Border Security Force Academy,

Tekanpur, Gwalior, in the state of Madhya Pradesh.

1967 – 1970: 2nd in Command and Chief Instructor, at National Cadet Corp (NCC) College

for Women, Gwalior, in the state of Madhya Pradesh

1970 – 1971: Officer Commanding, at 12 UP Girls NCC Battalion, Meerut, in the state of Uttar Pradesh

1971 -1972: 10211 War Dead Registration Unit (during Indo-Pakistan War), raised this Unit and served in Bangladesh

1972 – 1974: Commandant and Chief Security Officer, 16th Battalion, CISF, HEC, Ranchi, in the state of Jharkhand.

After his retirement from active service, he worked on welfare programs supporting retired servicemen and war widows in his native village, Jalari, district Hamirpur, in the state of Himachal Pradesh and subsequently was appointed as Vice-President of the state's Ex-Servicemen league.

For his distinguished service, he was decorated with the following medals:

- Waziristan Operation Medal (1937-38)
- Star (1939-45)
- War Medal (1939-45)
- Pacific Star (1941-45)
- Independence Medal (1947)
- Poorvi Star (1971)
- Sangram Medal
- 25th Independence Anniversary Medal.

Shawline Publishing Group Pty Ltd

www.shawlinepublishing.com.au

Lightning Source UK Ltd.
Milton Keynes UK
UKHW011154100921
390348UK00011B/663